How Desolate Our Home Bereft Of Thee

Sue Jensen Weeks was born in Provo, Utah. After attending public schools in Lewiston, New York and Palo Alto, California, she attended the University of Utah, University of Oslo, and Rhode Island School of Design. Sue has lived in Norway, Scotland and New York. She lives now in Salt Lake City.

How Desolate Our Home Bereft Of Thee

James Tillman Sanford Allred and the Circleville Massacre

SUE JENSEN WEEKS

Clouds of Magellan | Melbourne

First published 2014

ISBN: 9781742984681
ISBN – eBook: 9781742984698

Clouds of Magellan,
54 Woolton Avenue, Thornbury VIC 3071, Australia
www.cloudsofmagellanpress.net

A CiP record for this title is available from the National Library of Australia.

Cover photographs: James Tillman Sanford Allred, author collection; Paiute 'shades' – shelters – on the outskirts of a town, courtesy of Paiute Indian Tribe of Utah, Cedar City, Utah.

All publisher profits from the sale of this work will be donated to the Paiute Cultural Preservation Fund (Paiute Indian Tribe of Utah).

For my parents

Neldon and Kathleen Jensen

Contents

Introduction

MY GRANDMOTHER CARRIE LAFERN JENSEN loved to tell me stories.

Grandma Jensen was 4' 9" tall, had a halo of grey hair, blue eyes and always wore handmade aprons hanging on a nail by the telephone in the kitchen. The telephone number has never been changed since the phone was installed. The house smelled like butter, cream and bacon. The coal stove stood in the kitchen where grandma warmed her arthritic hips. After sledding behind the two toned green 1948 Chevy my uncle and father would drive through town, we would open the oven door and put the pillow with Chinese designs on the door and warm our feet. The mahogany radio sat in the west window.

Two hats hung by the east door to the kitchen. The coal shed was just east of the kitchen. The buggy shed and barn were located in the barnyard north of the house. The feeding trough was in the front of the barn. When we ate in the kitchen we could watch the black and white Holstein cows and the Percheron workhorses eat from the trough. There was an empty log cabin to the southeast of the farm and another on the block west.

Grandpa Daniel Lamont Jensen was a silent man who spoke mainly to his animals. Grandma Jensen was loquacious and loved visiting. She told me when she was young she and her sisters Edna, Sarah, Aurelia, Leah, and Ethelyn would often see Indians at their Grandpa Allred's house. They would come home at night from the dances and would have to walk around the block to get home as the Indians were camped in their Grandpa's yard.

"You see we lived right here and grandpa, why he lived just on the corner and we'd have ta go clear round the block ta get home there were so many Indians sleeping at his house. You see he could talk the Indian talk and that's why they'd come ya see ta get something ta eat. Why they'd be clear 'round the block and I think if they'd treated the Indians right in the first place there wouldn't a been so much trouble."

*

My father and mother have passed away since I began researching and writing this book about James Tillman Sanford Allred, based on family photographs, stories and family records.

What started as a project recording and compiling this information into a biography expanded into a twenty-year project after I learned about the involvement of my ancestors in a massacre of Paiute in 1866 in Circleville, Utah. Few knew about this, including many family members. Throughout the years, my Grandmother Jensen related anecdotal history about mistreatment of Native Americans.

I met with Paiute Elders twice and read from my manuscript. I listened as they told their historical accounts. During this process I gained insight into their intelligent, sensitive and democratic culture.

I write on a twenty-year old computer in a room with my Grandmother Jensen's alarm clock, my father's alarm clock and my favorite photographs of my parents and children. I inherited James Tillman Sanford Allred's mahogany mantel clock. A clock ticking was often the only sound in my Grandmother's quiet house. When I was four years old she took me with her to deliver Sunday dinner to my great grandfather, Daniel Jensen. He asked me if I knew how to tell time and explained how a clock worked.

On our annual Memorial Day pilgrimage to the Spring City Cemetery, my father became a raconteur for the deceased telling facts and stories and insights and opinions and sometimes simply who had the bad knees he inherited. My sons would complain but persevered in the generally early summer heat as we placed the current floral favorite of white, yellow and purple chrysanthemums instead of the peonies, bridal wreath and lilacs used by previous generations.

My father passed away in the room where he was born. My mother passed away in the same room. His cousin, who was ninety years old when she passed away this summer, wanted to proofread this manuscript.

I hear several clocks ticking this early autumn morning including my silver framed clock decorated with delicate numerals reminding me of my hard-working parents, their interest in knowledge, and the gift of time.

Sue Jensen Weeks, November 2014

… In November 1855 I returned home got my wife and 4 children and returned to Las Vegas, one son Edward was born there, we stayed two years then returned to Ephraim. I was called *showits* by the Indians. In 1864 I was called on a mission to Circle Valley. My wife died there April 20, 1866 after giving birth to a baby girl. We were the parents of 10 children. On account of Indian trouble my wife was buried the day she died. Me and my children returned to Ephraim in 1866 and then went to Spring city in July I bought a home and 73 acres of land. I served as a major in the Black Hawk War and held many responsible church positions. I have been a heavy user of chewing tobacco after hearing one of the apostles talk about using it I told my family I wouldn't use it any more. I have kept my word I began eating hard tack candy which I bought by the buckets Full. All the children liked it too. They called me "Candy Grandpa". I married my wifes sister Margaret, we had 5 children. She died Oct.10, 1888. My third wife was an Indian girl. We had 3 children. My fourth wife and I had no children.

I bore my testimony today Dec. 21, 1902 in Sacrament Meeting. I told the people that I had been personally acquainted with the Prophet Joseph Smith from 1834 to 1844. I played ball and wrestled with him. I have stood on my head on the top tower of the Nauvoo Temple and also on the Manti Temple.

—James Tillman Sanford Allred, aged 72 years, Spring City, Utah.

1

In April 1866, James Tillman Sanford Allred, and his son, Edward Francis Allred, were on their way home after getting supplies in Great Salt Lake City when they were met thirty miles south, at the point of the mountain, with the news that his wife, Eliza, was dying. James T.S. Allred gave his son, Edward Francis Allred, a six-shooter pistol and a horse to ride more than 200 miles to Circleville, Utah, so he could see his mother before she died. He would follow with the supplies. She died April 20, 1866, and was buried the same day due to tensions between the settlers and the Native Americans. A newborn baby girl survived her. Edward Francis Allred was ten years old in April 1866. Five months previously, Edward Allred, his brother, three sisters and two brothers-in-law had witnessed and survived an attack by Native Indians near the settlement of Circleville, Utah.

My father tells me that Edward Francis Allred liked to play baseball and didn't like to farm. He worked as a teamster driving wagons between Spring City, Utah and Las Vegas, Nevada. He was born in Las Vegas, Nevada, September 5, 1856, while his father was serving on a Mission as an Indian interpreter for the Mormon Church. Edward Francis Allred was James T.S. and Eliza Bridget Allred's sixth child, second son and the first child born to immigrants in the Nevada Territory.

His farm was southeast of Spring City, Utah, where the Allred's moved in June of 1866, after Brigham Young ordered the evacuation of Circleville because of the difficulties the settlers were having with the Native Indians. The farm is nestled on the east side of the valley below

Horseshoe Mountain. Canal Creek runs on the west side of the farm. The Manti La Sal Mountains rise more than 9,000 feet on the east side of the farm. He quarried the rough cut cream limestone for his home and built his home on the same block south of his father's log cabin on the fifth block south and first block east of the intersection of Center and Main Streets. Generally towns and cities took a church or a temple and numbered their streets from that point north, south, east and west. Center Street runs east and west and Main Street runs north and south.

The eight room Spring City Schoolhouse is located on Center Street and the Spring City Co Op, candy and ice cream store, City Hall, post office and gas station are located on Main Street. Our family farm is five blocks east on Center Street.

Edward Francis Allred farmed forty acres raising alfalfa and wheat, left forty acres in sagebrush and pastured his dairy herd on twenty acres in the wetlands west of town, which had a spring and a pond, and was where the children ice skated in the winter. He sold milk and eggs and later social security helped with his living expenses. Edward Francis Allred worked on the Mormon Manti Temple, walking nineteen miles from Spring City to Manti, staying a week and walking back. He married twice. His first wife died in childbirth leaving a daughter. He and his second wife had six children. After his second wife died in 1935, he spent three months of the year with each of his four daughters who lived in Spring City. Edward Francis Allred died July 11, 1942. He left his farm to his daughters and the pasture to his son. After selling the farm, each of the five daughters got $400. My grandmother bought a brown wool rug with pink flowers on it with her portion of the inheritance.

My father tells me that Edward Francis Allred was short, no more than 5' 5", thin and feisty. He often wanted to settle disputes by fist fighting. He had a moustache and he had blue eyes. From the few photographs we have, he looks like his father, though shorter. My father tells me when his grandfather was older and a widower living with them, he wouldn't let them read the sports page until he had finished. One time he got so angry he threw their black cat, Schwartz, through the north window in the kitchen. He continually complained about my father and his brother wasting food and wanted their mother to save the food they hadn't eaten for the next meal. He was a very thrifty person. Whenever a dance was held, he would buy one ticket and go for the first half of the dance then go home and his wife would attend the second half.

His nickname was "Cy Puss" as he would begin his sentences with "I says, says I" which contracted to "Cy" and "Puss" was added as a tribute to his horse, "Puss". He claimed that he could kill grouse in the mountains by hitting them with rocks. He had a tremendous throwing arm and would stand on the east side walk by the school house and throw a baseball 450 feet over the school house to the west side of the street.

Edward Francis Allred drove a Model T Ford automobile and one day while making a left hand turn on Main Street east to his home he collided with the egg truck. He became very angry and said to the driver, "Good God, what's wrong with you? Everyone knows I turn on this corner and it's your fault and you must pay." The egg man never paid. Edward Francis Allred had to hire a mechanic to straighten the front end of his car. He had a plum tree bordering the fence line. He noticed someone gathering plums on his side of the fence. The neighbor said that the plums that fell on his property belonged to him. Edward Francis Allred became irate and cursed him replying, "I guess you also own all the air in the air too." When Edward Francis Allred was once asked how he got away after being boxed in a canyon by some Native Americans, he said, "I didn't. They killed me."

*

I do not know all the traits James T.S. Allred had in common with his son, Edward. I do know that he shared an interest in wrestling and fist fighting, was feisty and had a slight build being about 5' 8" tall. After the Mormon Temple was completed in Nauvoo, Illinois, it wasn't just the heavenly spirit that moved Allred but a little of the earthly variety as well and he was so full of the bottled spirit that he climbed up to the temple steeple and stood on his head. James T.S. Allred was called the Candy Grandpa because he always had a little hard tack in his pocket he would share with the children. The hard tack also helped assuage his tobacco habit. When his grandchildren challenged him as an old man, he proved his youth by jumping over his horse. He knew and often met with Native Americans. One meeting took place soon after several settlers had been murdered. James T.S. Allred often rode alone twenty or thirty miles a day through desolate county on one errand or another. Some say that he was a spy for Brigham Young and others say that he was an opportunist who would defy Mormon doctrine to benefit himself. Others say he was a great man who helped forge the Mormon west. He had known relative frontier comfort in his parent's home on the Mississippi River and the hardships of living in wagons and dugouts.

James T.S. Allred must have been strong willed, determined, complicated, brave, weak, pugnacious and he must have had tremendous energy. He was educated enough to write a decent sentence in good script. He and his sons were handsome men with sharp blue eyes. In his daughter's account, written when she was eighty years old, she states, "I weighed 135–140 pounds and measured five feet. My eyes were grey and my hair black." I do know that they shared traits from their southern heritage and the peripatetic, uncertain life of early Mormon converts and early Utah settlers. They felt a certain privilege at being some of the first western pioneers, settling four towns in Utah and one in Nevada. They were also part of a clan, with many of them traveling west as the American Frontier expanded. Many members of the family converted to Mormonism and migrated to Utah. The Allred family to this day ranks as one of America's largest family trees. It includes Native Americans and African Americans. One branch, the James Allred family and his son, James T.S. Allred eventually settled in Spring City, Utah.

Spring City is a small farming town in central Utah. It is a high mountain valley at about 5,000 feet above sea level. It was once declared a ghost town with the population declining from a high of 1135 in 1900 to 456 in 1970. In 1890, 1044 people lived in Spring City and in 1990 there were 715 people living in Spring City. The population of Spring City has grown recently as people are interested in renovating the old homes listed on the National Historic Registry as well as participating in rural life once again. People make their living as dairy farmers, sheepherders, teachers and, in recent days, as turkey farmers. The town was first designed around an irrigation system bringing water from the mountains. The Native Americans stopped and used the springs on their migrations through the valley. The water from the springs is not enough to grow the crops needed to sustain the town.

It is a typical Mormon settlement with the houses in town having enough acreage to grow a vegetable garden. The farmland is located on the perimeter of the town. The town was divided into the section settled by the Allred's and others who came from Tennessee west with the Mormon exodus and Little Denmark where those from Scandinavia, especially Denmark, settled. The Allred's came first and got the best farmland. My grandmother was an Allred and my grandfather was a Jensen, a second generation Dane. Our family farm is on Center Street, right in the middle of Little Denmark on the north and the Allred section of town on the south.

A central village where families were close together helped to protect the settlers from attacks from enemies, which had been a constant threat to those of the Mormon faith from their beginnings in Palmyra, New York in 1830, with six original members of the faith. Mormons were persecuted for some of their "peculiar beliefs" and for their insular communities. But most distasteful to the rest of America was their practice of polygamy.

When James T.S. Allred was met at the point of the mountain with the news that his wife was dying, it was news that the first of his three wives was dying. He later married a fourth wife.

After his mother Eliza died, Edward Francis Allred was raised by his father's second wife, Margaret Mainwaring Roberts Allred, and briefly by his father's third wife Fanny Shantaquint, who died in the same year as Eliza.

*

Eliza Bridget Mainwaring Allred was born in Presteigne, Herefordshire, England on November 23, 1821. Presteigne was on the English and Welsh border in the Marsh Lands. Presteigne is now located in Wales as the border has changed several times throughout the centuries reflecting the turbulent history of the area. Presteigne sits in beautiful rich lowlands and rolling hills three miles east on the English side of Offa's Dyke (Clawdd Offa), an earthen mound twenty-five feet high and eighty miles long running north and south built by King Offa in the eighth century AD.

Eliza Bridget Mainwaring would have walked narrow cobblestone streets in a small thriving village surrounded by farms. She would have heard Welsh and English growing up although there is no evidence she spoke Welsh. Her family would have been poor with fewer prospects than had they been wealthy landholders. There are no Mainwarings buried in the churchyard. There is a small town, Nash, south of Presteigne, which is the maiden name of Eliza's mother.

Her family was not listed among the major landholders in Presteigne in the mid-1800s. The limited prospects for her class as well as her religious beliefs led her to immigrate to America. Eliza Bridget Mainwaring converted to Mormonism in 1835. Her sister also converted to Mormonism and joined her in America. Eliza Bridget Mainwaring converted to the Mormon Religion in England and came to America in one of the first groups of English converts. She worked for three years as a cook in Joseph Smith's household in order to pay off the debt to the Mormon Church she had incurred for her passage to America. Joseph Smith first promised Eliza Bridget Mainwaring to another man, Orson Hyde. Eliza Bridget Mainwaring had lived with the James Allred family where she met and fell in love with his son, James Tillman Sanford Allred. They lived kitty corner from Joseph Smith. She was released from marrying Hyde, and Eliza Bridget Mainwaring and James T.S. Allred were married November 23, 1845, in Nauvoo, Illinois, a bustling Mormon city on the banks of the Mississippi River. James T.S. Allred was twenty and his bride, Eliza, was twenty-four. Together they had ten children. Eight survived infancy. The children were:

Fent F. Allred
Eliza Marie Allred
Ellen Aurelia Allred
Elizabeth Diantha Allred
James Tillman Sanford Allred, Jr
Edward Francis Allred
William Hackley Allred
Nancy Cluny Allred
Brigham Young Allred
Margaret Bridget Allred

The children were born near Pueblo, Colorado; on the way west with the Mormon Battalion; in Las Vegas, Nevada; in Great Salt Lake City; Ephraim; Manti; and Circleville, Utah.

We have no photographs of Eliza Bridget Mainwaring Allred. She left no written records. She was small in stature and had brown hair, blue eyes. She must have been desperate, brave or trusting in her faith to make the journey to America. It is certain that she was brave once she got to America given her adventures and journeys throughout the west. She must have been accepting and open to the strange beliefs her religion required regarding polygamy. She was born in beautiful farmland and died in beautiful farmland. In between, the events of her life were remarkable. James T.S. Allred removed her body from the Circleville cemetery and brought her body on a wagon to Spring City for reburial. She rests beside two other wives and her husband. The inscription on her tombstone reads "How Desolate Our Home Bereft Of Thee".

2

EDWARD FRANCIS ALLRED MARRIED SALLY BILLINGTON and after she died he married Elizabeth Overlade, whose Danish family had a home in Fort Ephraim and later on Main Street in Ephraim. Her father, Andreas Jensen Overlade was known as "the flying carpenter" as he worked so quickly and also because there were so many Scandinavian immigrants with the same last names it was necessary to distinguish one from another. He was a carpenter and cabinetmaker who built homes, furniture and coffins. My father, his grandson, remembered him as being "small and agile and self-confident". Elizabeth, born October 27, 1861, was one of thirteen children. Her mother, Karen Marie Anderson Overlade, was a seamstress, a skill Elizabeth learned. She was a beautiful, dark haired woman who later in life suffered several strokes. She is said to have had a pleasant disposition and a keen sense of humor. She valued education and was concerned that her children do well in school. She married Edward Francis Allred October 20, 1884, when she was twenty-three years old and Edward Francis Allred was twenty-eight years old. They resided all their life in Spring City, Utah, where my grandmother, Carrie Lafern Allred was born.

Carrie Lafern Allred Jensen was born in Spring City, Utah, April 11, 1896, to Elizabeth Overlade and Edward Francis Allred in the oolite limestone house her father had built down the block from her grandfather, James T.S. Allred. Both houses were on the south end of town and commanded a grand view of Horseshoe Mountain. After marrying my grandpa, Daniel Lamont Jensen, March 27, 1918, she lived the rest of her life on the Jensen family farm on Center Street.

She gave me a copy of James T.S. Allred's daybook that had been stored in the chest painted a deep ox blood that her Grandfather Overlade had made. The glass knob handles on two of the four drawers are missing. The diary had been copied on white lined paper and was in the top drawer with her other prize possessions—an optometry kit my uncle had used during World War II which contained lenses and a glass eye, baby clothes, scarves, a hair net with small cultured pearls, hand crocheted doilies, a black cape with sequin border and green lining, a photograph of her brother, a pair of sparkling blue earrings, a compact with a crystal flower on top, obituaries held together with rubber bands, articles cut from the newspaper that she had saved to read to her grandchildren. On top of the chest was a layer cake of handmade quilts, an electric blanket, pillows, and bed sheets.

Grandma Jensen worried about the cold. She gave me the copy of her grandfather's diary for safe keeping as one of her other memory books had disappeared from the place and she was worried that something might happen to this account of her family's history. She told me she wouldn't take a hundred dollars for her father's chest and I mustn't either. Would I promise to take good care of the copy of her grandfather's diary and the chest? And I mustn't sell the chairs or the washstand or eagle legged table that belonged to her grandparents, Eliza Bridget and James T.S. Allred.

*

James T.S. Allred was born March 28, 1825, in Farmington, Bedford County, Tennessee to Elizabeth Warren and James Allred.

The first Allreds came from England, arriving in North Carolina around 1750. They were nonconformist Protestants and Quakers. Thomas, William, Solomon and John Allred were landowners in North Carolina by 1751. These immigrants came to Utah after settling in the Carolinas, Georgia, Tennessee, Kentucky, Missouri, Illinois and Iowa. William and Elizabeth Thrasher Allred had twelve children, William

Hackley, Martin Carrol, Hannah Caroline, Sally, Isaac, Reuben Warren, Wiley Payne, Nancy Chummy, Eliza Maria, James Tillman Sanford, John Franklin Lafayette and Andrew Jackson Allred.

While living in Missouri, they met missionaries from the Mormon Church and were converted from being "new school Presbyterians" to the Mormon faith, which had been founded in 1830 in the town of Palmyra in upstate New York by Joseph Smith based on a translation of symbols on golden plates using the Mormon Rosetta Stone, the Urim and Thummim. The Book of Mormon related the events of the lost tribe of Israel, which had immigrated to America. Joseph Smith had attempted to establish a home for his religion in Kirtland, Ohio. The early members of the Mormon Church were from New York, Vermont, Ohio and Kentucky. The pattern for Mormon persecution began early. The "saints" as they called themselves after their proper name, The Church of Jesus Christ of Latter Day Saints, had built their communities around their temples and tabernacles. They were mobbed. They were tarred and feathered. They would move onto the next "Zion" and begin again with their ranks swelling with their proselytizing and diminishing with their moving. They considered themselves a unique and chosen people.

James T.S. Allred was baptized February 22, 1835, at the age of ten years old. The Allreds were early converts to the Mormon Church and helped build the first Mormon communities of the Salt River Branch, Ralls County (later Monroe County), Missouri, known as the "Allred Settlement", which is a few miles southeast of Florida, Missouri, birthplace of Samuel Langhorne Clemens, who was born on November 30, 1835, as Halley's Comet blazed through the sky. The same phenomenon had a different meaning for James T.S. Allred's cousin, Reddick Newton Allred, who wrote in his diary, "the night the saints were expelled from their homes, the western world was shocked by the star falling from heaven that lit up the whole universe." In 1835, they moved to Little Fishing River, Clay County, Missouri, northeast of Liberty, Missouri. James Allred owned about 160 acres.

They then removed to land along the Log Creek in Grant Township, Caldwell County, Missouri. Clergymen denounced the Mormon Religion. Growing numbers of Mormons arrived, buying the land causing friction. The original Mormons came mainly from New England and were antislavery. They were accused of trying to free the slaves in Missouri. In 1838, Missouri Governor Boggs issued an extermination or expulsion order for Mormons living in the state of Missouri. People were shot and property was burned. Arrests were made. Joseph Smith ordered the members to go to Far West, Caldwell County, Missouri.

The Allreds lived outside the city of Far West but moved into the city at Joseph Smith's command for better protection. On November 1, 1838, while members of the Mormon Militia were out of town, the Missouri Militia entered Far West vandalizing the town and taking prisoners to Richmond. The rest of the Mormons were told to evacuate the state of Missouri. Those taken prisoner included Joseph Smith, James T.S. Allred's brother, Martin Carroll Allred, James T.S. Allred's uncle, William Allred and Andrew Whitlock. They were tried November 11, 1838, and charged with murder, arson, burglary, robbery and high treason against the state. November 24, 1838, twenty-three of the defendants, including the Allreds were released. On November 28, 1838, the trial ended. Joseph Smith and others were taken to Liberty Jail in Clay County, Missouri. Some prisoners were left in Richmond Jail. After six months, all prisoners were either released or had escaped.

After returning to Far West the Allreds signed a covenant:

> … to stand by and assist each other to the utmost of our abilities in removing from this state, and that we will never desert the poor who are worthy, till they shall be out of the reach of the exterminating order.

Three hundred and eighty people signed this document. Twenty-three years later, on February 17, 1861, Brigham Young addressed members in the Salt Lake Tabernacle and stated Missouri's Senator Thomas H. Benton had been responsible for the extermination order.

During February, 1839, Brigham Young and Heber C. Kimball, who were two of the Mormon twelve apostles, led the Mormons out of Missouri to Quincy, Illinois where they were warmly received. James and Elizabeth Allred moved their family to Pittsfield, Pike County, Illinois, residing most likely in the area on top of Fields Hill called Mormon Town. After Joseph Smith escaped from Missouri and was living in Commerce, later called Nauvoo, Illinois, petitions and affidavits for redress were presented to President Martin Van Buren. James Allred petitioned for his losses amounting to $2,000. Van Buren's unsympathetic response was, "Gentlemen, your cause is just, but I can do nothing for you."

In the fall of 1839, James and Elizabeth Allred, with three of their sons still living at home, James T.S. Allred 15 years old, John Franklin Lafayette Allred 12 years old and Andrew Jackson Allred 9 years old, moved to Nauvoo, Illinois, a town on the east side of the Mississippi River. They purchased an acre city lot for $250 from Joseph Smith near the banks of the Mississippi River. It was located on the southwest corner of Main and Sidney Streets. Joseph Smith's two-story log cabin, The Homestead, was just down the block. James Allred's assessed valuation of his property was $559, which included horses, cattle, a wagon, clocks, watches, the lot valued at $400 which included outbuildings as well as his home. This indicates he was one of the more fortunate members of the early settlers in Nauvoo. Brigham Young, John Taylor, Orrin Porter Rockwell, Heber C. Kimball, Wilford Woodruff and Orson Hyde among others lived nearby. The city was organized into eleven wards, or political districts, and functioned as the cultural, religious and social units. Farms were located outside of the city as well as across the river in Iowa. It was a bustling river town well situated for commerce.

*

On July 10, 1840, James Allred along with three others were kidnapped by seven men acting under orders from H.M. Woodward. Woodward and his band crossed from Missouri into Illinois taking James Allred and Noah Roger. Two days before, they captured Benjamin Boyce and Alanson Brown. All were incarcerated in Tully, Lewis County, Missouri, where they were held without warrant, beaten and tortured. On July 12, 1840, they were released with the statement, "The people of Tully having taken up Mr. Allred, with some others, and having examined into the offences committed, find nothing to justify his detention longer and have released him. Signed by order of the Committee, H.M. Woodward." Petitions from Mormons and non-Mormons circulated in protest of this action and were sent in vain to the Governor of Illinois.

S.M. Bartlett, who was a "gentile" as the Mormons called non-Mormons, describes James Allred as a "very respectable old gentleman, whose grey hairs should have protected him from insult." James Allred, a former county judge in Missouri, apparently addressed his captors firmly enough as to his rights that he was freed. However, in Bartlett's account, Alanson Brown confessed to stealing the goods precipitating the incident. The Mormons retorted that the confession by Brown was coerced and false.

On February 4, 1841, the Nauvoo Legion was authorized by the Illinois State Legislature and required to perform the same military functions as other state militias. James Allred was appointed Lieutenant General on Joseph Smith's personal staff as one of twelve bodyguards serving from 1841 until Smith's death in 1844. James Allred also served for five years as Supervisor of the Streets.

James T.S. Allred was appointed a 1st Lieutenant in the Nauvoo Legion September 28, 1844. He received his first command December 14, 1844.

In 1841 work began on the Nauvoo Temple where Mormons could perform their sacred ceremonies. According to Eliza Marie Allred Munson, Eliza and James T.S. Allred's oldest daughter, her mother, Elizabeth Allred, helped Joseph Smith's wife, Emma, design and sew what would become undergarments which at first "were made from unbleached muslin and bound with turkey red and were without collars". Garments are worn by all faithful members of the Mormon Church in the belief they protect the wearer from harm and for ceremonial purposes.

The town of Nauvoo was growing and prospering and was the second largest city in the state. The Mormons were virtually autonomous having received a charter from Illinois empowering them to organize a militia, the power to pass laws not in conflict with state or federal laws and have their own courts.

By 1844, church membership had grown to 35,000 members. The Nauvoo Legion numbered 4,000 men ready to obey Joseph Smith's orders. Joseph Smith ran for President of the United States.

Mormons constituted a strong and unified political force. But Joseph Smith had been practicing the doctrine of polygamy since 1841, and that coupled with the influx of Mormon converts coming to Nauvoo caused such antagonism that martial law was declared. Critics attacked Smith in print accusing him of being too dictatorial. Smith burned the press in response. Joseph Smith and his brother often went into hiding. Food was left out at night for the brothers including bread, buttermilk and potatoes warmed in the coals of the fire from the kitchen of James and Elizabeth Allred.

On June 24, 1844, Joseph Smith made his last speech to the Nauvoo Legion, admonishing them to protect Nauvoo and the Mormon inhabitants. Smith queried, "Are you not my boys?" and went on to ask, "Are you willing to die for me?" "Yes." "I will die for you. If this people cannot have their rights, my blood shall run upon the ground like water." He had received Governor Thomas Ford's pledge in good faith he would be protected by the state militia. He surrendered with his brother, Hyrum Smith, William Richards and John Taylor, saying, "If my life is worth nothing to you I will return, but I go as a lamb to the slaughter." Joseph Smith also went with the intention of leaving Illinois and going to the Rocky Mountains to find a place for his followers to live. Cynics in the crowd accused the men of being cowards and abandoning their fellow Mormons to the mercy of the mob.

On June 27, 1844, Joseph and Hyrum Smith were murdered in Carthage Jail, Hancock County, Illinois. While imprisoned, Joseph Smith gave his sword to James Allred saying, "Take this, you may need it to defend yourself." According to Reddick Newton Allred's diary, "Uncle James Allred went and hawled in the bodies next day with a small guard and the saints viewed the remains of the two great men of the 19th century. After which they were privately buried, while boxes representing their caskets were buried in the grave yard. The public never knew where they rested." On July 2, 1844, James Allred brought John Taylor, who had been wounded while imprisoned with Joseph and Hyrum Smith and William Richards, home to Nauvoo. Concern over his condition and the eighteen miles to be covered led the party to place a mattress on a sleigh behind James Allred's wagon. They took the most direct route home cutting through the fields and taking down fences. A crowd of thousands cheered their return.

After Smith's death, divisions developed within the Mormon community. Some believed in primogenitor and wanted Joseph Smith's son to lead their church. Others quarrelled over the doctrine of polygamy. Joseph Smith's first wife and son formed the Reorganized Church of Jesus Christ of Latter Day Saints. Splinter groups ended up in Texas and Wisconsin, as well as many other places.

On August 8, 1844, while speaking to members of the Mormon Church, around sixty people witnessed what they believed was Brigham Young's transfiguration into the appearance, voice and gestures of Joseph Smith. This was taken as a sign that he should assume the leadership of the Mormon Church.

The task of completing Nauvoo Temple was accomplished during this burly Vermonter's leadership. The four thousand pound capstone was laid on September 23, 1844. Nauvoo had built a foundry, a china factory, two steam driven sawmills, a steam driven flourmill, a tool factory and a steamboat. The town's craftsmen produced fired bricks, baked goods, guns. The farms produced grains and hay for livestock and vegetables and fruits for the townspeople.

The summer of 1845 brought increased attacks on the Mormon community especially on their leaders. The Nauvoo Temple was guarded beginning September 16, 1845. Despite the unsettled climate in Nauvoo, work had continued on the temple and was completed in 1846, just before their forced evacuation from Nauvoo. In January 1846 a circular was issued informing the Mormons that they should prepare to leave Nauvoo. James T.S. Allred writes that his father left Nauvoo on February 7, 1846. The Nauvoo Temple was looted and burned. Brigham Young, who was called "The Lion of the Lord", was to lead his band of followers on their exodus west.

The members of the Mormon Church formed an insular community. They traded only with members of their religion, when possible, and viewed religion and government as one and the same. Joseph Smith, followed by Brigham Young, were civic and spiritual leaders. They established their own government based on Mormon doctrine, had their own militia for protection of their religious city state, which given the history of the American Revolution was heretical. One of the basic premises of the constitution of the United States was the separation of church and state. Another view presents the Mormons as an extremely successful social order based on shared community property. In The Book of Mormon, King Benjamin says:

> And behold, I tell you these things that ye may learn wisdom; that ye may learn that when ye are in the service of your fellow beings ye are in the service of your God.

The rapid growth from Mormon converts emigrating, the financial success, the insular nature of Mormon communities and the practice of polygamy once again caused conflict. The Mormons sought a new Zion far from "gentiles", where they could practice their beliefs in peace. After reading Fremont's description of the Great Salt Lake Basin,

Brigham Young decided this place would become their destination. The Mormon Church placed great demands upon its members. Once again the chaff was separated from the wheat. Brigham Young stated:

> My people must be tried in all things, that they may be prepared to receive the glory that I have for them, even the glory of Zion, and he that will not bear chastisement is not worthy of my kingdom.

Some 16,000 Mormons were spread across 300 miles on the way west. At 5 AM a bugle called the members to arise and pray and begin the days' chores. At 7 AM another bugle called the camp to move the wagons and livestock. They stopped to till the soil and plant crops for those following to harvest.

On May 21st, 1846, Eliza and James T.S. Allred and three of his brothers started west to meet their father. James Allred and other family members had started February 9, 1846, and had arrived three months earlier in Pisgah, Iowa. From Pisgah, Iowa, they moved to Council Bluffs, Iowa, or "Winter Quarters", where their temporary living conditions were severe. Hundreds had died on the way. Their wagons were loaded with everything they needed to create a new community in the west. Livestock was herded beside the impoverished group, some walking, some were riding in wagons tilting with pots, pans, barrels, chickens and furniture and children. Brigham Young's only prophetic vision involved the organization of this motley assemblage into groups of tens, fifty and one hundred being commanded by captains. The vision ended with "And so no more at this time." The great administrator and future urban organizer began formulating his vision of the new Zion. His visions were of an earthly design.

3

THE UNITED STATES GOVERNMENT DECLARED WAR on Mexico, May 2, 1846. While living near Council Bluffs, Iowa, Captain James Allen of the United States Army brought a request to Brigham Young for 500 volunteers to form a Mormon Battalion. In three weeks the battalion was formed. The formation of The Mormon Battalion served several purposes. It came as a response to Brigham Young's request to the federal government offering their services in exchange for aid to the Mormons after their forced evacuation of Nauvoo. Brigham Young did not want to antagonize the federal government, which under President James Polk had signed a secret extermination order if they did not comply, and the Mormons could use the soldiers' pay as resources for the Mormon Church.

With the move from Nauvoo and subsequent loss of property and resources from their enterprises and the increase in membership, as many converts were coming from Europe without funds for their passage, the church coffers were low. The members of the Mormon Battalion sent their pay and clothing allowances worth $20,000 back to the Mormon Church. The Mormon Battalion also had permission from the federal government to camp on Indian reservations, making the trip west somewhat easier. The Mormons became players in the Polk Administration's Manifest Destiny Policy helping to push the United States boundaries westward to the Pacific Ocean. The United States Government had extended its hand to the Mormons hoping to ensure their allegiance to the federal government rather than to the Mexican, British or French governments.

The Mormon Battalion carved out many of the trails used later by pioneers expanding the western territory. Brigham Young wrote of the Mormon Battalion's contribution to its people, "This people must have perished had not these men gone into the service of their country. These men were the saviors of this people and did save them from carnage and death."

James T.S. Allred enlisted July 16, 1846, in Company A of the Mormon Battalion and they started their march from Council Bluffs, Iowa, July 21, 1846 as the band played "The Girl I left Behind Me". A ball had been held the night before. His wife, Eliza, was one of the twenty women allowed to go along as laundresses. James T.S. Allred was in the company of his cousins Reddick Newton Allred and James Riley Allred, his nephew Reuben Warren Allred and Elzadie Emeline Ford Allred, wife of Reuben Allred. Marching in front of the Mormon Battalion was a regiment of cavalry from Missouri, under Colonel Price, "of mob fame" writes Reddick Newton Allred. Mormons had previously encountered violence in Missouri and had been driven from Missouri to Illinois before their exodus west. Reddick Newton Allred proudly reports that the Missouri Calvary "didn't make as good time as we did", nor was a salute fired upon their arrival in Santa Fe as had been done for the Mormon Battalion.

When The Mormon Battalion arrived at Fort Leavenworth, Kansas, they were issued firearms, supplies and soldier's pay of $42. Most of the money was used by Brigham Young to aid families traveling west from Illinois. On August 12th, 13th and 14th, the five companies left Fort Leavenworth, Kansas for Santa Fe, New Mexico, under the stern command of Lieutenant A.J. Smith. After crossing the Arkansas River on September 16th, a detail of ten men took a number of families considered too weak to continue and settled them near Pueblo, Colorado, where they were to spend the winter. Eliza and James T.S. Allred continued on with the battalion towards Santa Fe, New Mexico. The Mormon Battalion covered about 15 miles a day for 61 days covering the distance of 900 miles between Fort Leavenworth and Santa

Fe. Poor rations, heat, the hard pace and sickness being treated by a doctor prescribing calomel and arsenic for every ailment, soon took their toll. According to Reddick Newton Allred's diary, if a soldier failed to complete the day's march, "they were compelled to report to Dr. Sanderson and take his caloline or querine otherwise they couldn't get to ride but must walk and do camp duty besides let them be ever so feeble."

On October 18, 1846, James T.S. and Eliza Allred along with one hundred and twenty-one others, including his nephew Reuben Warren and Reuben's wife, Elzadie Emeline Ford Allred, were ordered to Pueblo under Captain Brown and winter there with the Sick Detachment. Eliza and James T.S. Allred arrived with this group November 17, 1846. Their first son, Fent F., was born and died en route to Pueblo, Colorado. The party could not wait for James T.S. Allred to bury his son so he fell behind and arrived later in the evening exhausted from the experience.

Three hundred miles out of Santa Fe, New Mexico, the Battalion commander, Lieutenant Colonel P. St. George Cooke ordered another group of 150 of the weakest and sickest back to Pueblo to winter until spring. Cooke wrote of the Battalion:

> Everything conspired to discourage the extraordinary undertaking of marching this Battalion 1,100 miles, for the much greater part through an unknown wilderness without road or trail, and with a wagon train. It was enlisted too much by families, some were too old, some feeble, and some too young; it was embarrassed by many women; it was undisciplined; it was much worn by traveling on foot, and marching from Nauvoo, Illinois; their clothing was very scant; there was no money to pay them or clothing to issue; their mules were utterly broken down … and mules were scarce … those procured were very inferior, and were deteriorating every hour for lack of forage or grazing. I have

> brought road tools and have determined to take through my wagons; but the experiment is not a fair one, as the mules are nearly broken down at the outset.

Crude shelters were built to house the party during the winter described by traveling British officer George Ruxton in 1847:

> In a wide and well-timbered bottom of the Arkansas, the Mormons had erected a street of log shanties, in which to pass the inclement winter. These were built of rough logs of cottonwood, laid one above the other, the interstices filled with mud, and rendered impervious to wind or wet. At one end of the row of shanties was built … a long building of huge logs, in which prayer-meetings and holdings-forth took place.

There were 275 Mormons eventually quartered in Pueblo, Colorado. There were fifteen deaths. There were five births and two infant deaths. May 24, 1847, orders were received to journey on to Fort Laramie, Wyoming. On June 11, 1847, Amasa M. Lyman and others from Winter Quarters delivered mail carrying news from loved ones and instructions from Brigham Young. The detachment traveled through Wyoming, coming within 530 miles west of Council Bluffs, Iowa, their original point of departure. The party rested a day on the Platte River getting wagons repaired and animals shod taking advantage of a blacksmith in residence. Brigham Young's party arrived in the Salt Lake Valley on July 24, 1847. In a speech on July 27, he detailed his vision of the settlement:

> We do not intend to have any trade or commerce with the gentile world … The Kingdom of God cannot rise independent of the gentile nations until we produce, manufacture and make every article of use, convenience, or

> necessity among our own people … I am determined to cut every thread of this kind and live free and independent, untrammelled by any of their detestable customs and practices.

On July 29, 1847, Eliza Bridget and James T.S. Allred arrived with the Mormon Battalion's Brown's sick detachment in Salt Lake City, Utah five days after Brigham Young's party had arrived. They were released from the Mormon Battalion as their year of service had transpired. The main branch of the Mormon Battalion continued on to San Diego, California, covering over 2,000 miles and becoming one of the longest infantry marches in United States history.

Although the Battalion never engaged in battle, encountering nothing more than a herd of rampaging bulls, they proved critical in securing Colorado, New Mexico, Utah, Nevada, Arizona and California as the United States Western Frontier. Of the 350 men, 4 or 5 women, 25 wagons and 6 cannons that left Santa Fe, New Mexico on October 19, 1846, 5 of the original wagons and 335 men arrived in San Diego on January 29, 1847. Twenty men died en route. The Mormon Battalion camped at the Mission de Alcala while Colonel Cooke reported to General Kearney in the Casa de Bandini in "Old Town" San Diego.

On January 30, 1847, Colonel Cooke congratulated the Battalion saying, "History may be searched in vain for an equal march of Infantry." The Mormon Battalion was an army of occupation as the United States flag had been raised over San Diego on July 29, 1846. The men of the Mormon Battalion set to work building Fort Stockton as well as working on community development projects. They dug 15 wells, whitewashed homes. They brought their knowledge of making fired bricks with them and built the first fired brick building in California as well as lining wells with bricks to protect the drinking water. About 80 members of the Mormon Battalion remained in San Diego making up most of the non-Hispanic or non-Native American population.

One company remained in San Diego while others marched under General Kearney's command and built Fort Moore in Los Angeles. After the men of the Mormon Battalion were discharged, 81 men reenlisted. A messenger from Great Salt Lake City met the group informing them that most of their families had arrived in Salt Lake Valley and, "You will meet the Church in the Valley of the Great Salt Lake on the east side at the foot of the Mt." Upon arrival in Great Salt Lake City, a jubilee was held in honor of the members of the Mormon Battalion where Brigham Young declared, "These men were the salvation of this Church."

One hundred and six members of the Battalion traveled to Fort Sutter. James Marshall discovered gold January 24, 1848, on the banks of the American River as part of a group contracting for John A. Sutter building a gristmill and sawmill. Marshall described the event:

> It was a clear, cold morning; I shall never forget that morning. As I was taking my usual walk … my eye was caught with the glimpse of something shining in the bottom of the ditch. There was about a foot of water running then. I reached my hand down and picked it up; it made my heart thump, for I was certain it was gold.

"It was these Mormons boys that did it," reports Reddick Newton Allred. Ironically, the discovery of gold by "these Mormon boys" placed what Brigham Young had hoped would be an isolated Mormon utopia in Utah squarely on the path of of the California gold rush. Americans embraced the concept of Manifest Destiny, "54–40 or fight". The northern boundaries extended north to Canada and now Americans had extended the western boundaries to the Pacific Ocean. Americans viewed not only the physical boundaries as their domain but many also considered the destiny of the Native American and Hispanic people to be their province.

The Treaty of Guadeloupe Hidalgo of 1848, which ended the Mexican American War, embraced the Utah Territory as part of the United States and Brigham Young and the Mormons were once again forced out of the wilderness of Zion into the arms of the federal government. The clash between Mormons and gentiles would try both parties for generations.

The Mormon Battalion marched 2,000 miles under a flag written as "Bata lion", emphasizing their loyalty to their leader, Brigham Young, the Lion of the Lord. There are twelve stars on the flag they carried. Let there be no misunderstanding that they served their prophet and the twelve apostles above all others. They carved the trail that later would become the route for the Butterfield Stage Lines, and eventually became the route for the Southern Pacific Railroad.

The land selected for the Gadsen Purchase was selected using maps made by the Mormon Battalion. True to the promise made by Brigham Young at the outset of the Mormon Battalion's march, they never engaged in battle with the enemy. As recorded by Reddick Newton Allred, Brigham Young stated, "Go and you shall have no fighting to do. You shall go before and behind the battles." The only injuries any members received during their period of service were sustained when rampaging bulls charged the men and animals injuring three men and killing three mules. At least nine wild bulls were killed in the melee.

The men serving in the Mormon Battalion were paid:

Captain—$50 plus 20 cents per day for rations
1st Lieutenant—$30 plus 20 cents per day for rations
2nd Lieutenant—$25 plus 20 cents per day for rations
1st Sergeant—$16
2nd Sergeant—$13
Corporal—$9
Musician—$8
Private—$7

Some were paid with tools or livestock or seed aiding the Great Salt Lake City settlers establish their new community.

4

JAMES T.S. AND ELIZA BRIDGET ALLRED and others from the Allred family first settled at the mouth of Big Cottonwood Canyon near Big Cottonwood Creek, which flows out of the Wasatch Mountains to the east. Their first daughter, Eliza Marie, who claimed to be the second white child born in Great Salt Lake City, was born February 28, 1848, after the arrival of the Mormon pioneers. Patty Sessions, a midwife in the valley, records the event in her journal: "Monday 28 Put Eliza wife of James Alred to bed with a daughter born 12 PM."

James T.S. Allred started making adobes to supply the settlers with building materials; the two thousand saints who arrived in the valley the first year would need homes. Ten to twelve thousand were expected from Iowa and Nebraska. There were around twenty-five thousand Mormons but Brigham Young needed more for his western Utopia in the desert and escalated the missionary efforts worldwide sending missionaries to France, Italy, Scandinavia, South and Central America, the Sandwich and Solomon Islands, India. Expanding membership and expanding his boundaries occupied his vision. The Perpetual Emigration Fund financed the Mormon converts travel to Utah.

In 1850 The United States Congress created the Territory of Deseret from a parcel of land annexed from Mexico in the Treaty of Guadeloupe-Hidalgo. Deseret is a word taken from the Book of Mormon meaning honeybee, which symbolized the Mormon view of communal cooperation necessary to build their Zion in the west.

By 1849 Brigham Young was appointed Governor of the Utah Territory and Superintendent of Indian Affairs and by 1855 Brigham

Young had taken control of territory larger than the state of Texas. He hoped for Mormon Church controlled skipping stones all the way to the Pacific Ocean.

In May of 1849, James T.S. Allred and ten others were asked by Brigham Young to return to the Platte River in Wyoming and build a ferry to aid the migration of the Mormons coming west. They ferried seventy wagons a day at the rate of $4 per wagon. He earned $1,000 from this venture and returned to Salt Lake City outfitted with two wagons, four yoke of oxen, four cows, a heifer, a good supply of seed wheat and other articles discarded by immigrants at the ferry. Allred returned to Utah the same year where he was called by Brigham Young to help start a settlement in central Utah, one hundred and thirty miles south of Salt Lake City in Sanpete County.

James T.S. and Eliza Bridget Allred moved one hundred and thirty miles south to Manti, Sanpete County, Utah, in November of 1849. He took a whipsaw and a good supply of seed with him. The first winter was severe and he fed most of the seed to the livestock. He lost nine head of stock. In the entire community only 113 of 240 head of cattle survived. The Indians ate the livestock that died. Eliza and James T. S. Allred lived in a dugout on the south side of the hill where the Manti Temple now stands. Their second daughter, Ellen Aurelia Allred, was born in Manti, Utah, January 13, 1850. They were joined in October of 1851 by his parents, James and Elizabeth Allred, whom they had not seen in five years.

James T.S. Allred wrote of his early life in Manti and Ephraim in his journal. Daily life revolved around planting crops, taking care of the family and protecting the community from Native Americans. Building a cohesive community proved challenging as well, as there were rifts in relationships between the settlers and their various cultures. Resources for infrastructure were limited. Sometimes James T.S. Allred had the time to write in his daybook and then there are long pauses where he writes nothing. Here is an excerpt about his early years after he arrived in Great Salt Lake City:

In the spring of 49 I went back to Platt River to establish a ferry I was gone three months on my return I was called by Pres B. Young to go to Sanpete Valley to make a new settlement. I went in Nov 49 and in the winter of 49 and 50 we had so much snow that it killed most of our cattle. Jan 13 1850 my second daughter was born Ellen Aurelia. I settled in the south part of Sanpete Valley and in the fall of 51 my father and family arrived in Sanpete from the states I had been from him over 5 years. In Feb 23 1850 my oldest sister Hannah died leaving a husband and seven children and July 19 1850 my brother John Franklin Lafayette died leaving a wife and 1 child living and 1 dead he died with the colery. I remained in Manti City until the spring of 1852 when according to the council of President Young Father and I moved 16 miles north and started a new settlement we remained there until the spring of 53 July 29 when the Indians drove all off our horses and cattle. we then left our homes and moved to Manti City and I built a house and in the fall of 1853 I moved back to the old place according to the council of Pres Young I remained there about two months and then we were called on to leave the place again and go to Manti City. Dec 17 1853 about 51 families the most of them was Danish and among them was my father and family and 2 brothers and their families and my wifes brother and Richard Mainwaring and wife and her brother in law Richard Roberts and her sister Margaret who had just come from England this last season which was the first of her relations I had seen she left all of her folks in England and came to Nauvoo in 1842 for the gospels sake I remained in Manti City in 1853 and then was told by Brigham Young to start a new settlement 7 miles north on Cotton wood or Pine Creek which was the 7 of Feb 1854 there was 50 men who started this which was called Ephraim and on March 25 1852

> my third daughter Elizabeth Diantha was born in Manti and on the 25 of Feb 1854 my first son James T. S. was born in Manti. We finished our fort wall Mar 1854 which was built with stone 8 ft high we afterwards raised it to 10 ft. I moved my family up to Ephraim April 1854 and at the spring conference 1855 April 6 I was called to go on a mifsion to Los Vegas new mexico to preach to the Piute Indians and to learn them the arts and sciences of civilized life I therefore went to Salt Lake and was set apart for that mifsion and blessed by Pres Orson Hyde. A blessing upon the head of James T.S. Allred given under the hands of Orson Hyde and Bishop David Evans on Sat April 25 1855 in the seventies council hall of Great Salt Lake City pronounced by brother O. Hyde and Brother Allred in the name of the Lord Jesus Christ we lay our hands upon thy head and confirm upon thee all thy former blessings that they may rest with increased weight and power upon thee and they mind and that thou mayest be full of the Holy Ghost and also of the light and truth amen.

On March 22, 1852, they moved to Canal Creek, eighteen miles north of Manti, where James T.S. Allred erected a log house that he had brought with him. The cabin was sixteen feet square and the logs had been numbered for easy assembly and were then covered with boards. It was first placed just south of the Canal Creek but was moved seven times in the first year. The settlement of Canal Creek was also called The Allred Settlement, Little Denmark, Springtown and finally Spring City due to the numerous cold water springs in the town. Brigham Young had met with James Allred encouraging him to "select a place for settlement in the Sanpete Valley where he could locate with his numerous posterity and kindred and preside over them".

James and Elizabeth Allred, James T.S. and Eliza Bridget Allred, their two daughters Eliza Marie and Ellen Aurelia Allred, James T. S.

Allred's brother, Andrew Jackson Allred, nephews George M. Allred, Charles Whitlock and James F. Allred and two adopted Ute Indian children were the first settlers in Spring City. Brothers Wiley Payne Allred and Reuben Warren Allred along with Andrew Whitlock, Eleaser King, a widow named Parker and her son Frank, Henry Oviatt and others arrived soon after. Additional members of the Allred family would later join the settlement.

Brigham Young based his organization of settlements upon Joseph Smith's Plat of Zion. This plan called for houses built close together ensuring better protection for the settlers. The farmland was allotted outside the village. After visiting the Allred Settlement in April 1853, Brigham Young wrote:

> … they had previously been to me not only to know if they might settle in San Pete, but if they might separate widely from each other, over a piece of land about two miles square, each having a five acre lot for his garden, near their farms.

James T.S. Allred had surveyed 100 acres in the summer of 1852, dividing land into acre lots. There were 90 acres fenced and 39 acres were planted with grain and vegetables for a fall harvest. The survey is contained within the town's current boundary. The following is a list of landholdings in the fall of 1852.

J.T.S. Allred 5 acres Lot 2 Block 1
R.W. Allred 10 acres Lot 1 Block 1
R.W. Allred 10 acres Lot 1 Block 2
J.T.S. Allred 25 acres Lot 3 Block 2
James Allred 35 acres Lot 2 Block 2
Mrs. Parker not given

Canal Creek, the largest supply of water, runs out of the Manti La Sal Mountains east of the Sanpete Valley. The valley was well supplied with water as Cedar and Oak Creeks also flowed from the mountains into the valley. James Allred and James T.S. Allred established a claim to Canal Creek in 1852 or 1853. The claim was never formally recorded and James and James T. S. Allred relinquished these rights. The water from Canal Creek would later be claimed by Spring City.

The rights to the land and to the fresh water springs in the valley immediately caused friction between the settlers and the Indians. In the summer of 1852, when the settlers were tending their first crops in the fields, three hundred Ute Warriors from Chief Sanpitch's band approached. James T.S. Allred greeted them in their native language. The greeting placated the Indians. The Sanpitch Indians called James T.S. Allred *Showits*.

Soon after settling in Spring City, James T.S. Allred and his brother, Reuben Warren Allred, bought two Indian children from a band of Ute Indians returning from a raid in order to save them from being killed or sold into slavery. James T.S. Allred adopted a boy he named Nephi and Reuben Warren adopted a girl he named Rachel.

After a severe winter in 1852–1853, food supplies were low. More settlers were coming to the Sanpete Valley taking more land and using more of the area's resources. Relations with the Indians were becoming strained. Brigham Young had decreed that there should be a stop to the Indian practice of trading in slaves, which was a considerable source of Ute Chief Wakara's (Walker) wealth and therefore his status within the Ute Tribe. In May of 1852, Brigham Young had warned the Allreds to build a fort "for the purpose of securing themselves against the attacks from the Indians which council was subsequently found to be very timely …"

This advice was not heeded for no fortification had been completed. The conflict between the white settlers and the Native Americans known as the Walker War of 1853–1854 began.

On March 28, 1853, Brigham Young formally organized the Mormon settlement into a Bishop's Ward. He called Reuben Warren Allred, Wiley Payne Allred and James T.S. Allred to preside over the colony. This colony did not last long for it was evacuated December 17, 1853. Even though James and his son Reuben W. Allred had requested and received in October of 1853 a newly arrived contingency of Danish immigrants to help fortify the town, it was not enough and the settlers left for Manti and the protection of the fort located there. On December 3, 1853, Governor Young offered amnesty to all warring parties and stated:

> If the Indians will all be quiet and friendly, I will try to induce my people to furnish them bread, clothing, and other articles for their comfort, and some powder and lead to hunt with, but I shall want the Indians to work for what they get from the whites, as we had to do, or pay in skins, and quit begging.

On July 20th 1853 at 20 minutes after 11 o'clock, the following message was written:

> Lieutenants James T.S. Alred, Gardiner G. Potter. Sirs you will meet bringing your affects and familys at the Alred post if it should meet the views of the companys commanded by you. you will consolidate and fortify yourselves at that place but the two settlements or either of them may come to this place at their option and if one settlement comes let the other come also I send six men all that can be spared at this point at preasent to assist pleasant creek post in moving and guarding their familys & affects as above. W. Higgins commanding Sanpete Military district.

Brigham Young wrote directly to Chief Walker on July 25, 1853:

> Capt Wacher,
>
> I send you some tobacco for you to smoke in the Mountains when you get lonesome. You are a fool for

> fighting your best friend for we are the best friends and the only friends that you have in the world. Everybody else would kill you if they could get a chance. If you get hungry send some friendly Indian down to the settlements or come your self and we will give you some beef cattle and flour. If you are afraid of the Tobacco which I send you, you can let some of you prisoners try it first and then you will know that it is good. When you git good natured again I should like to see you don't you think that you would be ashamed. You know I have always been your best friend.

Brigham Young signed his letters in a large sprawling signature ending with a flourish on the "g".

In 1853, Report No. 3 from Sanpete Militia District, Manti, N. Higgins states:

> Sir I have the honor to report that since my last report organised and spyes have been constanly on duty but made no discoveries. At 4 O clock PM Lieut JTS Allreds report of date July 23rd 8 O clock am nothing of importance. July 23rd 5 O clock PM another report arrives from Lieut. JTS Allred reporting that two Utah Indians had came in to his Post appparently friendly one of them well known by the name of Is he states that he saw a dust on the 22nd about 5 O clock PM: which he supposed to be Walker crofsing from Petnet Kenyon to Uwinta Vally. he further says that Utah Indian by the name of Fattswoods stole and drove off two head of cattle from this place on the 21st he dos propose piloting a company of Mormons to Walkers bait but I did not send any troops after him. He often would contradict himself so that all confidence was lost in what he said. I ordered said two Indians to be kept overnight then to go and tell the Indians they could come back and be friendly if they wishe so to do

> but not to be prowling about in the night if they did our people would shoot them.

Report No. 3 lends credibility to the belief that James T.S. Allred was part of an organization of "spyes" created within the nascent communities but what their purpose was is uncertain. Were they to spy on fellow Mormons to see that their lives were being lived according to religious doctrine or was this group formed for a military purpose concentrating on the perceived threats from the Native Americans?

In Report No. 6, August 2, 1853, Manti, Utah, from Head Quarters Sanpete District Nauvoo Legion and Utah Militia N. Higgins writes:

> Liet J.T.S. Allred reported to me today on his arrival at this place that at the same time the Indians drove off the cattle from his post a party of the Indians plundered his fathers Jas. Allreds house a short distant from the fort which house had been evacuated the day previous leaving considerable furniture the most of which was carried off by the Indians.

Report No. 11 from Fort Manti, October 25, 1853 to James Ferguson Head Quarters Sanpete Dist. Nauvoo Legion & Utah Militia reads:

> Sir I have the honour to report that since my last report of the 5th nothing of importance has transpired. On the 21st I ordered Lieut JTS Allred to enrole all the men at his post as many strangers had settled at that place and the most of the form setlers had returned as per cancil from the Governer. Lieut Allred's report has just arrived he reports sixty one men able to bare arms and only two horses one sadle twenty nine guns one hundred and thirty rounds of ball and only four and a half pouunds of powder to the whole sixty one men. These

> men are mostly Danes and are very poor so if arms and ammunition could be furnished I think they could defend the place I would be pleased if you could have thirty two guns and some powder & lead forwarded to this place for them. Lieut Allred reports Indian smoke in the neighbourhood Pleas order an election for company officers at the Allred post Also to fill the vacancy in their company at this place. Yours Truly, N Higgins Major commanding Sanpete Dist

Young's offer of good will and goods was ignored with hostile acts continuing until January 6, 1854. The Allred Settlement, Spring City, was burned, after settlers had returned without permission in October, following the evacuation the previous July. They were ordered to evacuate again in November. This act and the theft of a large herd of cattle near Spanish Fork on February 26, 1854 were the final acts of the Walker War.

On March 12, 1854 five Indians from Chief Walker's camp and one Mexican from Santa Fe came to Fort Manti requesting that a meeting take place at Chief Walker's camp on the Sevier River. Lieutenant James T.S. Allred and three other men with a wagon full of gifts left March 13th to meet with Chief Walker and returned at 5:30 in the morning on March 16th with the following report:

> Maj N Higgins,
>
> Sir agreeable to your order under date of the 13th Inst I with the detachment under my charge proceeded on my journey to Walkers camp when we had traveled about twelve miles I met Teweep Walkers brother who informed me that Walker had removed his camp twenty miles south of Salt creek in the Sevier vally which makes the distance from this place to his camp about fifty miles we arrived at willow creek in the Sevier Vally about 6 o clock next morning I with one Utah who I had with me as a guide left the waggon & three

men directing them to follow me at day light for Walkers camp which I reached about 9 o clock AM 15th I immediately requested Walker with some of his men to accompany me back to meete the waggon & three men as the team was tired and hevy loaded with provisions for him which request he readily complied with On my return with Walker and fifteen of his men I met the wagon & men Seven miles south of Salt creek here we halted and smoked the pipe of peace I then red a letter to him from Isaac or Father Morley with which he was well pleased he said Father Morley was a good man and had always treated him well he further said that he was Father Morleys friend he then put the letter into his bosom and said that he would keep it for he loved it and father Morley He said that our coming and bringing him the letter was in fulfillment of a dream which he had some time ago he then arose to his feet and prayed some five or ten minutes He then sat down and said he wished to talk over our difficulties and tell me what his feelings had been and what they are now he commenced at the time we came to this vally saying the Mormons about that time and the … Utes had some troubles and that the Mormons killed some of his friends yet it did not make him mad but some of his men became very mad and wanted to fight but he perswaded them to be at peace and that he has always since tried to keep them quiet and friendly to the Mormons and still wishes to be friendly but that it hurts him when the Mormons accuse him of being untrue and a liar which he says they do as he has heard. He says this last difficulty was caused by the mormons … to the assalt at Springvill or Hobble Creek the Indian that received the blow over the head in that affair was his cosin who has since died he says that made him a little mad and being blinded by the influence of the Dead and not seeing the result of the course he was taking caused him to act as he has

He more over sad at the time that Ivie struck the Indian Shaweneshockits with the gun that the Indian was whiping a Squaw which was no difference to the Mormons if he had of kill her but had it of been a Mormon woman that he was whipping then the Mormons would of been justifiable in interfiarn. From this offence they killed the man of Payson and stole some property he says that when he left Payson and got over the mountain he began to think and came to the conclusion that his men have done enough for that offence and told them so and tried to get them to hold on but they were determined upon more depredations and urged him to come down uppon the Allred & Hambletan settlements and kill them all off and drive their stock but that he perswaded them not to kill the people but be content with driving off there stock which they were determined on doing. Yet he was opposed to that but could not prevent them and as a proof he says that he made an alarm smoke so that the Mormons might get up their cattle.

He talked a long time amounting to nearly the same thing all the which justifying himself & pleading the cause of his people saying that we have taken his land and fishing places and now he wishes the Mormons to purchase his land and make peace. He wishes Gov. Young to send D.B. Hentingdon immediately to meete him at Fillmore to make a treaty with him and purchase his land. He also wishes him to send guns ammunitions & blankets to trade to him for horses.

He promises to be at peace until he hears from Gov. Young

Yours

JTS Allred

During the early months of the Walker War, Reuben Warren Allred's adopted daughter, Rachel, was visited by her natural mother who was on her way to the mountains. Her mother came to Rachel's window and warned Rachel that the Indians were coming to kill the settlers. Rachel became upset and told her adopted brothers and sisters the reason she was crying. The children were sent out to warn the town's people. She is credited with saving Spring City's residents from being killed. The settlers of Spring City were able to prepare for an attack of whooping and yelling but no stock were driven off nor were any people killed.

An early settler of Spring City recorded the event:

> … the Indians were stimulated in their ravages upon the approach of Winter which came with an abundance of snow, and a fierce and intense cold weather We left Spring Town to cover this distance in the midst of heavy snow storm.
>
> Practically all the emigrants who went to Manti for the winter went as a colony in the Spring of 1854 to a point about seven miles north of Manti … A fort wall was constructed of stone surrounding a tract on which the Ephraim Tabernacle and City Library now stand. The wall was about nine feet high and built of limestone which was hauled from the mountains Northeast of the fort. Port holes were provided near the top of the wall … Log and mud houses were built within the fort wall to provide for the settlers, many of whom lived in their wagons and tents … cattle were corralled in the center of the fort.

January 29, 1855, Ute Chief Walker died. On January 26, 1855, Arapeen, Walker's brother, and successor to Chief Walker deeded Sanpete County to the Mormons. The relationship between the Mormon pioneers and the Indians was complicated given that Mormon theology believes Native Americans, called "Lamanites" in the Book of Mormon, are one of the lost tribes of Israel.

So it was a complicated relationship that Brigham Young balanced between salvation and survival. Missives from Brigham Young show compassion as well as outright aggression toward the Native American population. In a letter from Brigham Young to Reddick Newton Allred, James T.S. Allred's cousin, dated April 14, 1865, Brigham Young states:

> They must be made to entertain a wholesome fear for our Justice as well as a feeling of respect and honor for our mercy.
>
> In the truth, I remain as ever,
> Your Brother, Brigham Young

James T.S. and Eliza Allred lived in Manti, Utah from December 17, 1853 through February 4, 1854. Their fifth child, James Tillman Sanford Allred, Junior was born February 25, 1854, in Manti Utah. It is seven miles between Ephraim and Manti and ten miles between Ephraim and Spring City, Utah. Spring City is on the north and Manti on the south with Ephraim in between.

Ellen Aurelia Allred, Eliza Bridget and James T.S. Allred's second daughter, describes their life:

> My father, James T.S. Allred and thirty other men went as Colonists, at the request of Pres. Brigham Young in the Fall of 1849, to what is now Manti, Sanpete County, Utah. Due to the lateness of the year, winter was approaching and it was getting very cold. So it was impossible to build cabins for the protection of their families through the winter months. So they were compelled to seek places around the foot hills where they could dig a place in the hill side large enough for a wagon box with a cover on it, to fit in. My father selected a spot on the south side of the hill, and almost straight down the hill from where the Manti Temple stands. He prepared the place and the wagon box was

placed in the excavation. So my wonderful mother related to me how happy my father was when he had such a nice warm place for his little family.

It was in one of these covered wagon boxes that my mother went down into the valley of the shadow of death to bring me in to the world, that cold morning the 13th day of January 1850. My father told me years later that he put pans on the bed to keep my mother dry, as the canvas cover would leak when it stormed. He also told me that I had a special duty to perform in this life, as the Lord had permitted me to be born at the foot of one of His Holy Temples.

In the spring of 1850 father built a fine log cabin, and there we lived until March 1852, when Pres. Brigham Young selected some of these settlers, to go north to Canal Creek and establish a settlement. My father hauled logs enough from Manti to build his cabin and his was one of the first completed in the settlement, and soon others were built, and they decided to call the new town 'Allred Town'. Later a company of immigrants come to the little town from Denmark, so it was decided to cal the town 'Little Denmark'. And at a later date Pres. Brigham Young said it should be called Spring City, for there were so many valuable springs with in the boundaries of the town. A fort was constructed for their protection from the Indians, crops were planted and many other improvements were made for their comfort and safety. When every thing seemed to be going ok the Indians raided the settlement stealing a lot of their cattle and destroying most of the crops. This misfortune caused them to return to Manti, to save their lives. In February 1854 My father was called to help settle Ephraim, eight miles north of Manti, where they

> erected a fort and this proved to be a permanent community.

Lush beautiful willows and grasses surround the natural springs for which Spring City is named. The Wasatch Plateau rises to 10,000 feet on the east. This is the source for most of the irrigation water the early settlers rerouted into irrigation canals and which was one of the early sources of conflict between the Native Americans and the white settlers. The mountains to the east are covered in Aspen and pine trees. The low foothills to the west are sagebrush covered. There are miles of cedar groves between Spring City and Ephraim where the deer winter. After a spring rainstorm, the smell of cedar pierces the air.

Jackrabbits, skunks, raccoons roam the fields. Bald Eagles perch in the Cottonwood trees and mountain spruces in winter. Owls, magpies, blue birds, doves, meadowlarks, blackbirds and hawks fill the clear blue sky above the valley. Thunderstorms roll across the valley in summer and scattered rainstorms can be seen from one town to another as grey filaments of water vapour float down from the clouds. The vistas stretch thirty miles. The puffy white cumulus clouds frame the sky. Sunsets are dramatic pinks and purple ribbons, interplaying with the sunlight shooting from the west and bouncing off the mountaintops.

Low hills rest between Spring City and Ephraim beyond the cedar grove. The road curves west. Ephraim is seven miles south and is not as close to the mountains as Spring City. The valley is flat surrounded on the east and west with putty hued foothills. There are marshes on the west where blackbirds nest and serenade in the evening.

Rows of poplar trees have been planted in Manti. On the east side of the valley are the foothills where the early pioneers built their "dugouts" and where later the Manti Temple was built. Pines planted by pioneer ancestors still guard the north entrance to Manti and frame the cemetery where many of the early settlers are buried.

At the extreme southern end of Sanpete County the land is drier and flatter than the northern end. The valley is open and wide. The mountains recede into the sculptural land of the southwest where Nature's pottery wheel has thrown red mud cliffs and caverns and mountains and valleys in myriad shapes.

5

BECAUSE OF THE THREATS FROM THE NATIVE AMERICANS, Sanpete Valley settlers were all housed in Manti during late December of 1853 and 1854. The fort was crowded and once again James T.S. Allred and fifty families were called to move north seven miles where they settled on the banks of Pine Creek or Cotton Wood Creek. This settlement was named Ephraim and was begun February 7, 1854. The original fort enclosed about one and one half acres and was built of stone ten feet high. The roof was made of logs, willows and dirt. The fort was completed in March 1854.

With the arrival of more people later in the fall of 1854, the fort was expanded to include an area 60 x 44 1/2 rods or about seventeen acres and the walls on the north side were raised to fourteen feet high and four feet thick on the top. In 1855 the fort was completed at a cost of $13,000. Allred moved his family to Ephraim in April of 1855 where he built the first cabin within the fort. He was in company with his father and mother, James and Elizabeth Allred and his brothers Reuben Warren Allred and Wiley Payne Allred.

A year after moving to Ephraim, Utah, on April 6, 1855, James T.S. Allred was called upon by Brigham Young to go preach the Mormon Gospel to the Paiute Indians in Las Vegas, Nevada. He was called to serve as an interpreter to the Native Americans being blessed by Orson Hyde in Salt Lake City. He left Ephraim on May 8, 1855, at two o' clock in the morning. He met with the company led by President Bringhurst May 29, 1855, near the Iron Works west of Cedar City, Utah.

James T.S. Allred was in the company of George W. Bean, a one armed colonist for the Mormon Church, who kept a journal of his experiences as a U. S. Marshal, Indian Agent and guide to many U.S. Army expeditions in the west during the years 1850–1870.

George W. Bean recorded his association with James T.S. Allred:

> May 13th Moved out at 6 ½ a.m. Got to Buckhorn Springs watered some of the animals then went on to the Meadow or Little Creek where we arrived at 3 p.m. good grass and water. 29 miles today. Heard that my sister was very sick & rode on to Parowan City arrived at 8 p.m. I begged the privilege of leaving the command here & waiting until the missionaries came on going to the Vegas. the Lieut. agreed that Jim Allred and myself could leave & paid us off.

Bean recorded that he was pleased to be rid of the U.S. Army and the feeling was mutual as the Lieutenant in charge of the federal troops, Lt. Maury, wrote in his report that he was glad to be rid of his two guides, Bean and Allred.

On June 16, 1855 at about ten o'clock at night, James T.S. Allred arrived in Las Vegas, Nevada, "safe and sound not loosing the first animal on the way to die which I think is a great blessing and also a merical." Allred's duties were making building adobes and gathering and whipsawing the lumber needed to construct the fort. The fort was one hundred and fifty feet square and made of sundried adobes placed on a stone foundation. The walls were two feet thick at the base and tapered to one foot thick rising to fourteen feet. There was one large door on the north side and peepholes to use for observation.

John C. Fremont wrote first account of European Americans stopping at the Las Vegas Springs when he took a cut off across southern Nevada. Arriving in Las Vegas was a 'merical' after trekking across the last sixty miles of Great Basin Desert with water scarce. They came to the "las vegas" or "the meadows", where one hundred acres of grassland fed on natural springs. A twelve-foot waterfall and a three-mile long stream form along a fault line. The stream went back underground near the mesquite field. To the east were eighteen miles of mesquite wood used for fence posts and firewood. The leaves of the mesquite bush were coated in rosin becoming fragrant after infrequent rainstorms. The waterfall became a source of power and the stream irrigated the crops.

James T.S. Allred's daughter Ellen Aurelia Allred Nielsen recorded her memories of life in Las Vegas in 1919 when she was sixty-nine years old:

> At the age of five I went with my family to Las Vegas, Nevada, where my father had been called on a mission to serve as an interpreter between the Indians and the white settlers. President Young was trying everything possible to get along with the hostile tribes in that area and to establish a feeling of peace and trust. Instead of so much stealing and murdering and bad conditions in that area. My mother worried so much about my father as he was in constant danger all the time, he had a very hard task to fulfill, the very hot weather and the hostility of the Indians were a very poor combination. My father was surely a Heaven sent blessing to these people and he never tired in trying to teach them how to work and get along with other people. My mother was wonderful she was at his side always ready to help in any way possible. She had some large kettles and she would fill them with porridge and soup and some days they would feed over a hundred Indians and their wives and children. Sometimes they were so hungry they would dip their hands into the kettles where the food was still scooping unable to wait until it had cooked. They were so ungrateful for everything but my father was so patient with them but very stern and never showed any fear of them. Father was a great wrestler and he

tried to show the Indians how to pass the time away with out fighting and killing. One night a very large group were there for supper and mother had all of the kettles full of good smelling food, when father told them that from now on the blessing was going to be said on the food and thank the Lord for His blessings. He had just finished talking when a very large Indian come over to one of the kettles and put dirty can in to get some soup and father called to him to wait a minute, and he didn't pay any attention but continued to fill his bowl, father spoke to him the second time and no answer, then my father grabbed him and threw him away from the kettles and the Indian landed on his back and when he regained his feet father grabbed him and threw him on his back again, this time as the Indian got to his feet, he drew a long knife and made a lunge at father, who stepped a side and grabbed his arm that held the knife and father twisted his arm until he dropped the knife and then father held on to him and talked to him till he had quieted down. Then my father told the group we will give thanks for the food and then you can have all you can eat. But no more unclean cans will be used to dip the food, now help your selves and see that your wives and children get all they can eat. Then he turned to the Indian that he had just given a severe lesson, and took him by the hand and led him to one of the kettles and got him a clean bowl and a dipper to get some soup. My mother said, that fathers success with Indians was that he could talk their language. My wonderful mother was so frightened the night of the fight, and when she told father how worried she was, my father gave her a hug and kiss with this promise, remember my Dear we are on a mission and our living prophet of the Lord, has gave us his promise that we will return to our home in safety, when our mission is over.

Aroet Lucius Hale, a fellow settler, wrote of his recollection of the Las Vegas Mission:

> If I remember correctly, the distance from Salt Lake City was 565 miles, the last 65 miles was from the Muddy to Las Vegas. There was very little water on the Great Desert, and though we traveled with ox teams, we lost no cattle. Mexicans told us that a like trip in that regard had never been known at that season of the year.

John Steele's reflections of Las Vegas are recorded in his diary:

> Monday 19th I went to work and plumbed the north star and got the range and laid out the fort 150 feet square, by the assistance of T.D. Brown. And the same day he left in company of Rufus C. Allen, Peter Shirts, and five others. Continued our operations and with the assistance of J.T.S. Allred and others succeeded getting some garden lots of 3 rods by 12 ½ laid, 30 in number; also 15 five acre lots making 2 ½ acres apiece for the company consisting of 30 men. Most of the brethren were in favor of 5 acres of land apiece, but owing to so much mesquite brush on it, it was found to be very hard to grub on account of the prickles on the bushes.

Steele continues:

> Nothing of any importance took place up to the 4th of July, which was celebrated with the greatest pomp and show on the evening of the 3rd. The captain of the Mission called us all together and said it was necessary for us to organize into a military company for the purpose of self defense, accordingly he motioned that I should be the captain of the company, which was voted and accordingly, although I was very

unwilling to accept of the office on account of a dream I had the night before that I was on top of a house nailing on the roofing boards and I was afraid, and when I was nominated for captain I had the same feelings precisely. James T.S. Allred was then appointed first lieutenant, Albert Napp, 2nd, William Follett 3rd, Roett Hail, 1st sergeant, and all the others officers.

*

On November 10, 1855, James T.S. Allred left Las Vegas, Nevada for Ephraim, Utah. He kept the following journal of his mission in Las Vegas.

Day Book of James T.S. Allred, May 8, 1855 to April 21, 1856.

Tuesday May 8th 1855—I left home about one or two o clock in the morning in Company with my brother Reuben and Charles Whittock and started on my mission that I was called to fill at the April conference 1855 being appointed to go to Los Vegas. I started to go with a company of U.S. Soldiers as an interpreter for them to go with them to Sanborndeno and I was to meet with them at Filmore City and my brother was to accompany me to filimore City. we traveled about 50 miles and camped on the south side of Round valley until about midnight

Wednesday 9th May—we started and traveled a little ways an met some horses that had stampeded from the soldiers the night before beyond Filimore. we arrived at Filmore about 9 o clock and I parted with my brother. he returned home and I went to meadow creek making 30 miles travel

Thursday 10th May—moved to corn creek 6 miles

Friday 11th May—we moved onto pine creek 27 miles good water and grafs

Saturday 12th May—traveled about 25 miles and camped on beaver creek grafs plenty

Sunday 13th May—we moved on to little Creek in Iron Co and the Comp Camped and that night I left them and went on in to Parowan Citty making about 28 miles we travelled. I left the train because they was so wicked and was cussing the Mormons all the time

Monday 14th May—I remained in Parawan and wrote a letter back to my wife

Tuesday 15th May—I went up into the canion along with brother I. Steel

Wednesday 16th May—I traveled on through Cedar City and went on down to Fort Harmony distance 35 or 40 miles

Thursday 17th May—I helped brother Dalton on the road

Friday 18th May—I helped him make a wagon box

Saturday 19th May—I plowed for him

Sunday 20th May—I went back to Cedar City and heard President Young preach a first rate sermon

Monday 21st May—I wrote another letter home and then went down to Harmony 18 miles

Tuesday 22nd May—I went down to where old Fort Harmony was to help wash wool

Wednesday 23rd May—I plowed for brother Dalton again

Thursday 24th May—I started back to Cedar Citty to meet the Company of missionaries I stopped on a small Creek called Shirts creek with Hyrans and Benson they was moveing to Harmony

Friday 25th May—I went on to the City and stoped at brother Hults

Saturday 26th May—I went up to the foundry and seen them casting

Sunday 27th May—attended meeting

Monday 28th May—worked for brother Hults

Tuesday 29th May—the Co arrived in this City

Wednesday 30th May—I resumed my journey along with President Bringhurst & co this day we traveled about 22 miles

Tuesday 31st May—we traveled 12 miles and camped at the mountain meadows

Friday 1st June—I traveled 8 miles with the Company and stoped to noon and here I got brother Willis to hawl about

300 lbs of my load and I went on in co with him and traveled about 15 miles and camped on the St ebClarry

Saturday 2nd June—In the morning we traveled 16 miles and stoped at a small cabin where we leave this river until an hour by sun where we started on and traveled 10 miles and camped on the divid between the virgin and St ebClarry

Sunday morning 3rd June—we traveled 20 miles and stoped at the cotton woodsprings near the Virgin in the afternon we started on and traveled down the Virgin river 12 miles crofsing it 6 times and stoped at the lower end of some cottonwood trees in the virgin bottom there was plenty grafs here In the morning ourhorses was gone back quite a peace

Monday 4th June—in the afternoon we traveled 15 miles

Tuesday 5th June—our horses 5 of them was gone again we found them about noon we started on and traveled 8 miles and camped where we leave the virgin this day we met a company of merchants from California on their way to Salt Lake

Wednesday 6th June—we arose early in the morning & climb the virgin hill the worst that I ever seen went up with wagons and traveled over to the Mudy and up to the Crofsing 22 miles. There we found plenty of Indians who appeared very friendly at dark we met together as usual for prayer and after prayers br R. Allen Pres of the St ebclarry Indian Mission who had traveled in company with brother Willis and co and my self from the St ebclarry … with four others namely J. D. Brown I. Riddle T. Haskels and P. Shirts they are on an exploreing expeditson to the Colorado River he arose and gave the

Indians some good instructions brother Willis also spoke to them through me as interpreter after wards three of the chieves spoke well and requested that we should baptize them and their people brother Allen accordingly told them to come together the next day and we would attend to the ordinance of baptism

Thursday 7th June—early the Indians comenced gathering together and about 9 o clock we opened our meeting by singing and prayer and then comenced baptiz ing untill we baptized 200 & 1 persons & confirmed them in one day & after wards there was good instructions unto them

Friday 8th June—br Willis Brown and myself visited the natives at their own lodges they received us kindly and offered us victuals to eat of their own manufacture for they farm considerable & raise wheat corn beans & squashes & co.—they appear to be very anxious for the mormons to come and settle with them but it is a poor chance for fire woods or timber to all appearance but they say that their is timber up the river ash and other timber within one days travel from here

Saturday 9th June—we baptized and confirmed about 30 more of the natives and brother Willis and comp started home with tolerable good loads of Iron that they had picked up which was their businefs out here and he didn't charge anything for halling for me or br Allen & Co …

Sunday 10th June—I still remain here waiting for the company of Los Vegas mifsionaries anxious for them to get along

Monday 11th June—early in the morning an Indian came and told me that they was close by br Allen and myself went back and met them they was coming very slow there teams some of them was allmost giving out as it was so warm and the roads was so sandy and bad they stoped awhile where they first stuck the mudy then in the afternoon roled on up to the crofsing with the intention to lay by a few days and recruit

Tuesday 12th June—two of the brethren an myself went up the mudy about10 miles and got some ash timber to make some yokes Wednesday 13th President Bringhurst started to crofs the desert with 9 of the best teams and left the rest of the company in my charge to start the next day at 9 1/2 o clock the same hour that they started

Thursday 14th June—I arose early and wrote a letter to send home when I should meet the mail and at 9 1/2 o clock we started and travelled slow all day it being very warm and the roads very sandy and a gradual rize for about 12 or 15 miles we stoped at 6 o clock a let our teams rest and graze an hour we then traveled all most all night and about 25 or 30 miles from the mudy we found good grafs for a desert and here we stoped about 3 hours and then roled on very slow. It being Friday 15th and warm and gradually up hill about 2 o clock we came on to a hill from where we could see our place of destination the Los Vegas country It fill my heart with joy to see it and also to see at the foot of the hill wagons and team and it loaded with about 300 galons of the Vegas water we here watered our teams alittle to each one and then rolled first rate untill we got within 6 or 8 miles of the water and then I started after and before I got to the camp I met Pres. Bringhurst with some teams to help us in we all got to camp about l0 o clock at night except one team and three men and br Meriams wagon we had to leave a few miles back on account of braking a tire and this day met the mail from California

Saturday 16th June—I arose early and found that the mail had arrived in the night from Salt Lake and I received a letter from my wife and I went back and helped fit in br Merriams wagon this day found us all at the Los Vegas safe and sound not looseing the first animal on the way to die which I think is a great blefsing and also a merical

Sunday 17th June—the mail started on and we built a shade for to hold meetings under in the after noon had a good meeting and voted that br S. Hanlet & G.W. Brown should go with br R. Allen & Co on to the colorado river exploring

Monday 18th June—The corner sloping was stuck for the fort and also 1/4 of an acre of land for each man was surveyed

Tuesday 19th June—I assisted in surveying out some five acre lots sixteen in number we drew for them two men for one lot

Wednesday 20th June—plowed alittle

Thursday 21st June—put in some seeds for the first

Friday 22nd June—put in some more seeds and cousin R N Allred arrived at our place this evening on his return home from a mifsion to the Islands

Saturday 23rd June—put in some more grain

Sunday 24th June—I wrote another letter home

Monday 25th June—I grubbed some and plowed a little

Tuesday 26th June—the company of mifsionaries left us 14 in number

Wednesday 27th June—I helped make the water main ditch

Thursday 28th Friday 29th Saturday 30th—I was grubing plowing and planting

Sunday 1st July—attended meeting Ira Miles was droped from his councilor ship to the president and G. Snider was put in his place and G.W. Bean was appointed clerk

Monday 2nd July—Sowed 1/4 of an acre of wheat

Tuesday 3rd July—plowed a little more and in the evening organized a Military Com I Steal Capt

Wednesday 4th July—at the dawn of day we fired off our guns and pistols and also the anvil we also raised a small liberty pole an a flagg with the stars and stripes on it at the Moment the flagg was unfurled we fired a salute and then gave 3 cheers we then repaired to the bowery and had some first rate speeches delivered and a few toasts and songs some of the songs was composed for the occasion

Thursday 5th July—we broke up 1/2 acre for peas

Friday 6th July—put them in

Saturday 7th July—I washed some clothes

Sunday 8th July—attended meeting

Monday 9th July—water corn and the Mail arrived from California

Tuesday 10th July—I wrote the 5 letters home

Wednesday 11th July—I watered my garden

Thursday 12th July—I herded the cattle

Friday 13th July—hoed some corn and potatoes

Saturday 14th July—I made me a shade

Sunday 15th July—I attended meeting about sunset Mr Higgins and Carter arrived at our camp from california

Monday 16th July—the mail arrived from Salt Lake with letters and papers for the most of the brethren but I received none

Tuesday 17th July—I wrote the 6th letter home and sent by A Higgins and in the afternoon President Bringhurst and 8 of the brethren started to explore for timber west

Wednesday 18th July—I hoed some corn

Thursday 19th July—President Bringhurst & co returned and reported that they found some good timber about 20 miles west

Friday 20th July—I made fence

Saturday 21st July—I made me a place to sleep on

Sunday 22nd July—attended Meeting

Monday 23rd July—I helped to make some bridges

Tuesday 24th July—I made some more fence and commenced the cattle corrall

Wednesday 25th July—worked at the correll and Thursday 26th also Friday 27th we finished our part of the corrall and had a dance at night

Saturday 28th July—watered some corn & potatoes

Sunday 29th July—attended meeting

Monday 30th July—hoed some corn and peas & Tuesday 31st another party started on an exploring expedition for timber

Wednesday August 1st 1855—plowed and hoed out some corn

Thursday 2nd August—I went to the Indians lodges and layed hands on nortompourefs the chieves distance four miles

Friday 3rd August—hoed Corn

Saturday 4th August—I worked in the garden and the exploreing party returned and reported plenty of timber with in 40 miles of this place Sunday 5th attended meeting

Monday 6th August—put in a few turnips

Tuesday 7th August—watered the gardens

Wednesday 8th August—sowed some more turnips

Thursday 9th August—hoed some peas

Friday 10th August—herded again

Saturday 11th August—cleared off an adobie yard

Sunday 12th August—attended meeting and wrote some

Monday 13th August—The Cal mail arrived and I finished my letters

Tuesday 14th August—I commenced making adobies

Wednesday 15th Thursday 16th—the Salt Lake mail arrived and to my great satisfaction I received two letters from home

Friday 17th August—I made adobies

Saturday 18th August—I wrote a letter to R.W. Allred in Cal and watered the gardens and made adobies

Sunday l9th August—I attended meeting

Monday 20th August—I got my mare shod and fixed to go after Iron

Tuesday 21st August—I traveled to the cottonwood springs 25 miles

Wednesday 22nd August—I travelled to the mountains springs 12 miles and then back

Thursday 23rd August—came back home with some iron and poles

Friday 24th—I made adobies & also Saturday 25th

Sunday 26th—attended meeting

Monday 27th Tuesday 28th Wednesday 29th—I made adobies and in the afternoon my team started after timber

Thursday 30th Friday 31st—we had green corn to eat & I made adobies

Saturday September 1st 1855—I watered my garden

Sunday 2nd—attended meeting

Monday 3rd—I stacked some adobies and worked 3/4 day public works

Tuesday 4th Wednesday 5th Thursday 6th—I whip sawed some lumber for the President And Friday 7th & Saturday 8th I sawed with the whip saw

Sunday 9th—attended meeting and hurded

Monday 10th—I got my oxen shod

Tuesday 11th—I divided my provisions and went into another mefs

Wednesday 12th—I helped to get the Comp started to california with our oxen and the California Mail arrived

Thursday 13th—sawed for the President

Friday 14th—the mail arrived from Salt Lake and I received one letter from home

Saturday 15th—I sawed for the President

Sunday 16th—I attended meeting in the forenoon in the afternoon I visited some Indians four miles below and gave them some instructions

Monday 17th Tuesday 18th Wednesday l0th Thursday 20th Friday 21st & Saturday 22nd—I whipsawed all this week

Sunday 23rd—I attended meeting and addrefsed some of the Lamonites and there was a company of men arrived here from Salt Lake

Monday 24th Tuesday 25th Wednesday 26th Thursday 27th Friday 28th—I whip sawed and Saturday 29th was my hurd day

Sunday 30th—I attended meeting and gave the natives some instructionz about stealing and I told them they must quit it

Monday Oct 1st 1855 Tuesday 2nd Wednesday 3rd Thursday 4th Friday 5th and Saturday 6th—I whip sawed

Sunday 7th—I guarded the field to keep the birds out

Monday 8th Tuesday 9th—I whip sawed and this day I delivered up the cows to J. P. Hirons that I had in my charge of C.W. Daltonz and Hirons left for California

Wednesday 10th Thursday 11th Friday 12th Saturday 13th—I whipsawed and this day we moved into our house and the California mail arrived after dark

Sunday 14th—I rote a letter home and the Salt Lake mail arrived about 12 o clock but did not bring any letterz for me this is the first time that the two mailz has met here since we arrived here

Monday 15th—A large drove of cattle arrived here on there way to California

Tuesday 16th—I whip sawed

Wednesday 17th—I traded my mare off for a mule and a cow and calf

Thursday 18th Friday 19th Saturday 20th—I whip sawed and to day there is a company here from California on there way to the lake

Sunday 21st—I hurded it being my herd day

Monday 22nd Tuesday 23rd—I whipsawed

Wednesday 24th—I cut up my corn

Thursday 25th—I drawed adobies

Friday 26th Saturday 27th—I worked at some sinches[1] for the bretheren

Sunday 28th—I attended meeting and we had a good meeting

Monday 29th—I guarded in the field

Tuesday 30th—I husked out my corn

Wednesday 31st—I worked on my wall

Thursday Nov 1st—I doctored my mule and talked to the Indians

Friday 2nd—was a very cold windy day and President Bringhurst arrived here from California with alot of mules & horses

Saturday 3rd—the animals was divided out and I received one horse & one mule and this morning my white mule die

Sunday 4th—I attended meeting and this day we baptized 66 of the natives and gave them a few squashes & co

Monday 5th—I worked at my briddle and larriette and sinches

Tuesday 6th—do–do

Wednesday 7th—I gathered my beans

[1] Cinches were spun from horsehair and were used to secure saddles.

Thursday 8th—I gathered squashes and this Friday part of our company started home to visit their familes and br Amasa Terman arrived here from California

Friday 9th—I was fixing to start home

Saturday10th of November 1855—I started home on visit and traveled 25 miles

Sunday 11th—2 o clock in the morning we started and traveled 12 miles and got breakfast then we traveled on to the muddy and down to where we leave it 16 miles making 28 miles here I got the Indians to guard the animalz

Monday 12th—we crossed over to the Riovirgin and up it 4 miles 22 miles here The Indians guarded the animals

Tuesday 13th—we traveled 8 miles and found good bunch grafs up a big hollow to the left 1 mile

Wednesday 14th—We traveled 10 miles the piedes hurded our animals the 2 nights

Thursday 15th—we traveled 13 miles & camped at the beaver dam

Friday 16th—we travelled 30 miles & camped at the little cabin on the St ebclarry

Saturday 17th—we traveled 18 miles

Sunday 18th—we traveled 15 miles & camped at the Mountain Meadows[2]

Monday 19th—I left Brother A Leiman & company & traveled 35 miles to Cedar City and here I heard from my family that they was destitute of bread stuff but all well

Tuesday 20th—I traded for 150 lbs of flower and traveled 6 miles to Fort Johnson

Wednesday 21st—I travled to Parowan & took dinner with br J. Steelz & then travelled on to the springs 26 milez

Thursday 22nd—I traveled 30 miles

Friday 23rd—I arose about 7 o clock in the morning & travelled about 5 miles and came to a camp of brethren from Sanpete that had been cedar City for provisionz I traveled to corn creek 35 miles this day it stormed all day

Saturday 24th—I traveled in to Fillmore City & took dinner with some brethren from Manti City & then traveled on to Unionville 24 miles

Sunday 25th—my mules ran away but after hunting awhile I found them I then travelled 26 miles and camped in the Severe River[3]

---

[2] Two years later on September 11 1857, Mormon settlers disguising themselves as Southern Paiutes attacked the Baker–Fancher wagon train at Mountain Meadows and killed around 120 men women and children—mostly settler families from Arkansas—in what is known as the Mountain Meadows Massacre.

[3] Sevier River.

Monday 26th—I started on before day and traveled 15 miles up the Severe and got breakfast then traveled on threw Manti City and arrived at Fort Ephraim about sun set making 47 miles and found my family all well in good spirits

Tuesday 27th—I visited around among my friends and relatives

Wednesday 28th—I went up to the coal bed to see it

Thursday 29th—my brother inlaw Francis Manwaring arrived at Fort Ephraim in good health and spiritz safe from England

Friday 30th—I spun some hair to make some sinches

Saturday Dec 1st 1855—I hawled some wood

Sunday 2nd—I attended meeting and gave the brethren a brief sketch of my travels

Monday 3rd—I spun some more hair for to make sinches and myself and family took supper at br G. Hills

Tuesday 4th—I was quite unwell

Wednesday 5th & Thursday 6th—I spun some hair for to make some sinches

Friday 7th—it was quiet stormy allday & I made 2 cinches

Saturday 8th—I made some more cinches

Sunday 9th—I attended meeting

Monday 10th & Tuesday 11th—I was busy making sinches & fixing to start to Salt Lake City on bufsiness

Wednesday 12th—I traveled to Nephi City 35 miles & found it very bad traveling

Thursday 13th—it snowed threw the past night and I learned here that the snow was one foot deep about summit Creek & roads very bad so I started home and arrived at Fort Ephraim

Friday 14th—after traveling all night Saturday 15th at home all day & my eyes was very bad having taken cold

Sunday 16th—attended meeting

Monday 17th—I acted as first councilor to the bishop on a trial between Reese & Thorpe Tuesday 18th

Wednesday 19th Thursday 20th—I was hawling wood for myself

Friday 21st—I put my hay upon my shed

Saturday 22nd—very stormy allday

Sunday 23rd—Sister Roberts little girl departed this life

Monday 24th—I went to Manti City

Tuesday 25th—I returned home and we had a dance

Wednesday 26th—I went ahunting

Thursday 27th Friday 28th Saturday 29th—I helped alittle to repair the school house

Sunday 30th—attended meeting

Monday 31st—at home all day

Tuesday Jan 1st 1856—we had another dance and also at night we had a first rate time

Wednesday 2nd—I hawled a load of wood

Thursday 3rd—I attended the fast meeting[4]

Friday 4th Saturday 5th—I hawled wood and this evening brs E Snow & G. B. Wallace arrive at Fort Ephraim to settle the difficulties of this branch and to reorganize it they spoke to us this evening in the school house and gave us some good instructionz

Sunday 6th—They held 2 meetings and droped the bishop and the president of this place and then went to Manti

Monday 7th—I went to Manti to meeting and then back home and attended meeting in the evening

Tuesday 8th—br Snow and Wallace returned and held another meeting at Eleven o clock and gave some good council to the brethren and they organized this branch of the church by Ordaining John L. Chase bishop and he is to preside over this branch and he chose James T. S. Allred to be his first

---

[4] Mormons are encouraged to fast the first Sunday of every month.

councilor & Paul E. Koford 2nd and they was unanimously sustained by the branch

Wednesday 9th—brs Snow & Wallace started back to Nephi City and it stormed some

Thursday 10th—I hawled a load of wood

Friday 11th—I hawled a load of wood

Saturday 12th—hawled wood

Sunday 13th—attended meeting

Monday 14th—I let the Indians have some 4 1/2 bus potatoes

Tuesday 15th—I worked in the tithing house[5]

Wednesday 16th Thursday 17th Friday 18th Saturday 19th—I was about home tinkering

Sunday 20th—I attended meeting and br Chase attended with us also

Monday 21st—we located aplace for a small City 1/2 mile square[6]

Tuesday 22nd—we celebrated my Fathers birthday by making a dinner for the connection in this place and a dance in the evening we had a first rate time of rejoicing

---

[5] Mormons believe in tithing. Some tithes were paid in goods held in tithing houses.

[6] Ephraim, Utah.

Wednesday 23rd—I was engaged in settling with bishop R W. Allred and it stormed very hard all day

Thursday 24th—we surveyed off the place for the meeting house & stuck the corner stakes

Friday 25th—I delt out 30 bushells frozen tithing potatoes to the brethren

Saturday 26th—at home all day

Sunday 27th—I attended meeting

Monday 28th—I fixed up my cow yard

Tuesday 29th Wednesday 30th Thursday 31st—I was halling some hay for father and myself

Friday February 1st 1856—I helped to make a hole through the fort wall for the water to run threw

Saturday 2nd—I spun some stuff to make some sinches

Sunday 3rd—I attended meeting

Monday 4th—I worked for I Edrusston

Tuesday 5th—I caled out the militia at fort Ephraim and drilled them and inspected their arms Maj N. Higgins met with uz

Wednesday 6th—I spun some hair to make some sinches

Thursday 7th—I attended fast meeting

Friday 8th—I made some sinches

Saturday 9th—I worked on the school house repairing it

Sunday 10th—I attended meeting

Monday 11th—I measured up some potatoes and was fixing to start to Salt Lake City

Tuesday 12th—I attended the high priests and Seventies[7] meeting and dance

Wednesday 13th—I consecrated my property and in the afternoon I started to Salt Lake City & traveled to Manti 7 miles

Thursday 14th—I traveled 32 miles and camped near the point of rocks on the severe in the Cedars

Friday 15th—I traveled 33 miles to Nephi City and attended dance in the evening

Saturday 16th—I traveled to Pason 25 miles

Sunday *17th*—I traveled on threw Palmira Springville Provo & on to Pleasant Grove 30 miles

Monday 18th—I traveled on threw American fork Lehi & on to big Cotton wood 30 miles

Tuesday 19th—I traveled on in to Great Salt Lake City 10 miles

---

[7] Members of the Mormon Melchizedek Priesthood called to serve as traveling ministers.

Wednesday 20th—I had an interview with President Young

Thursday 21st—I sold the right to my traveling fees and subsistence money to Judge Snow for 100 dollars in goods

Friday 22nd—I started home & traveled to Pleasant grove 35 miles

Saturday 23rd—I was hunting my horse in the fore noon & in the afternoon I went to Provo 12 miles

Sunday 24th—I remained in Provo City

Monday 25th—I bought some corn & wheat & I.W. Turner was hunting for my horse

Tuesday 26th—I found my horse & traveled to Payson 20 miles

Wednesday 27th—I traveled to Nephi City 25 miles & attended a dance

Thursday 28th—I traveled 8 miles up the Canion

Friday 29th—I traveled 8 miles snow very bad

Saturday March 1st 1856—I traveled 20 miles and arrived at Fort Ephraim my home

Sunday 2nd—I attended meeting

Monday 3rd—at home all day

Tuesday 4th—I worked on the stone quary

Wednesday 5th—I went to Manti to talk with the Indians and we gave them two fat cows

Thursday 6th—I wroth a letter to my brother Isaac

Friday 7th Saturday 8th—at home all the time fixing to start on my mifsion and Saturday I baptized my oldest daughter Eliza Maria

Sunday 9th—attended meeting & Father Allred I.D. Chase and myself confirmed Eliza Maria

Monday 10th—I was trying to trade for some provisions

Tuesday 11th—I was helping to lay up my fort wall

Wednesday 12th—I traded for 10 bushellz potatoes

Thursday 13th—at home waiting to hear from the Los Vegas company by letter

Friday 14th—I heard that they was a going to start as soon as the weather would permit

Saturday 15th—at home all day very stormy fresh snow fell about 6 or 8 inches deep

Sunday 16th—I attended meeting

Monday 17th—I traded a mule for a yoke of oxen

Tuesday 18th—I went to Manti to swap horses

Wednesday 19th—I worked on my old wagon

Thursday 20th—I inspected the arms of the Militia at Fort Ephraim

Friday 21st—I made a wagon tongue

Saturday 22nd—I helped to clean out the fort

Sunday 23rd—I attended meeting

Monday 24th—I helped to fix up the Publick Correll

Tuesday 25th—I spread some hemp to dry

Wednesday 26th—I broke some hemp

Thursday 27th—I broke & hetcheled some hemp

Friday 28th—I am 31 years old this day

Saturday 29th—I baptized 7 persons

Sunday 30th—at home all day

Monday 31st—I planted potatoes

Tuesday April 1st 1856—I broke some hemp

Wednesday 2nd—I made some bed cordz

Thursday 3rd—It was fast day

Friday 4th—I went to Manti to talk to the Indians

Saturday 5th—I made some sinches and ropes

Sunday 6th—at home all day

Monday 7th—helped to fix up Fathers wagon to start to the City

Tuesday 8th—I started to Salt Lake City & traveled to Migos springs 20 miles

Wednesday 9th—I traveled to summit Creek 35 miles

Thursday 10th—traveled to Battle Creek[8] 34 miles

Friday 11th—I traveled to Allens pasture 32 miles

Saturday 12th—I went into the City 4 miles and was sealed[9] to Mrs Margarethe Robertz

Sunday 13th—I started home and traveled to Lehi City 27 miles it rained very hard

Monday 14th—I traveled to Provo 20 miles

Tuesday 15th—I tried to trade for oxen

Wednesday 16th—I traveled to Springville

---

[8] Battle Creek—now named Pleasant Grove—Utah, was the site of one of the first organised attacks against the Ute in March 1849.

[9] Sealing Ceremony is performed in Mormon Temples.

> *Thursday 17th*—I traded my horse and mule for two yoke of oxen and travelled to the shonte quint springs 15 miles
>
> *Friday 18th*—I traveled to Nephi 24 miles
>
> *Saturday 19th*—I arrived at home 35 miles
>
> *Sunday 20th*—I attended meeting

*

George Mayer recalls his fellow missionary, James T.S. Allred, in his diary:

> We traveled through the different tribes of Indians without any trouble. The Las Vegas Indians sent some men with us to the Muddy Indians. They received us kindly and herded our cattle. We rested one day and left for the Rio Virgen and there the Indians were all friendly. We treated them as friends and made them flour mush, and put our cattle in their hands. They treated us as friends and took good care of our cattle, returned them all safe every morning. James Allred was our interpreter, they would attend prayer with us evenings, then we would sing hymns for them. Then they would sing for us in their language, they seemed to enjoy the spirit of the Gospel of Jesus Christ.

The Las Vegas Mission closed. James T.S. Allred was thirty years old and this was the fourth mission he had been called to serve for his faith. An endowment house had been built in the fort serving the settlers in their Mormon missionary work bringing their gospel to the Native Americans. When miners arrived to extract the ore needed for bullets in the surrounding hills tensions broke out between the miners and the missionaries. The Mormon's endowment house was destroyed.

Johnston's army was on Brigham Young's doorstep in Great Salt Lake City and the missionaries were called home. President Buchanan ordered 2,500 troops to escort a new governor, Alfred Cumming to Utah in order to install a new territorial government. Brigham Young declared martial law on August 5, 1857 and with Young's Nauvoo Legion numbering around 6,200 men war was expected. The newspapers were filled with sensational accounts of the Mormons in Utah. Mormon militia attacked supply trains and set fire to sections of South Western Wyoming. On September 11, 1857 a party from Arkansas traveling through Utah was massacred at Mountain Meadows in southern Utah. Johnston's Army encamped for the winter at Fort Bridger, Wyoming. In 1858 a peace commission negotiated an agreement and Alfred Cumming was seated as governor of the territory.

6

EPHRAIM WAS FIRST CALLED PINE CREEK. James T.S. and Eliza and Margaret Allred's cabin was the first built within the walls of the fort. The Allred's future daughter-in-law's family, the Overlades, also had a home inside the fort. There was also a church, school tannery, saw mill, bowery, tithing house, stone cutter's home and Seventy's Home. A stream runs around the perimeter of the inside wall. The seven foot walls enclosed a fort about one and one half acres. The first settlers included the families of James Allred, Reuben Warren and James T.S. Allred.

Many settlers from Spring City came to Fort Ephraim after being driven out by Native Americans. The first fort was built at a cost of $13,000 and completed in 1855. Ephraim was built a few miles north of a Native American burial mound placing it in the pathway of migration routes of the Ute Indians.

Building a community occupied daily life. There were fields to clear and plant and irrigation ditches to be dug. There were the leaders to elect. There were marriages, babies to be born and deaths. There were skills needed to keep a community going and religious observances of these Mormon pioneers attended to. James T.S. Allred kept the following daybook[10].

*

[10] The first entries given here for March-April preserve the original 'layout' of the daybook; from May onwards the text is laid out in a more 'reader friendly' style.

March 28th 1858 we received orders to raise 20 wagons and teams to go to Salt Lake City to assist in moving the poor south & Monday 29th I was fixing to go with my wagon & the team & Tuesday 30th we started with 23 teams & wagons we traveled to Cunaity springs 20 miles Wednesday 31st we traveled 25 miles Thursday April 1st 1858 we traveled 15 miles Friday 2nd we traveled to Provo City Saturday 3rd we traveled 20 miles Sunday 4th we traveled 20 miles & arrived at GSL City & I attended meeting in the afternoon Monday 5th I was attending to some business Tuesday 6th I attended the general Conference President B. Young presiding who spoke well brothers Kimble & Wells who spoke well & gave good instructions Wednesday 7th I started home & traveled to Provo 46 miles Tuesday 8th I traveled 15 miles it snowed very hard Friday 9th I traveled 12 miles it was very bad going Saturday 10th I traveled 20 miles going better Sunday 11th I traveled 30 miles & arrived at home Monday 12th fine weather all well Tuesday 13th I was unwell & also my wife Wednesday 14th beautiful day all well Thursday 15th Friday 16th Saturday 17th fine weather all well I was puting in some garden seeds & co—Sunday 18th all well I attended meting we had a good time some of the new comers spoke first rate Monday 19th Tuesday 20th Wednesday 21st I was busily engaged in seeding & co—Thursday 22nd I went to Manti Citty to get some ammunition for the jublie Friday 23rd Saturday 24th I was puting in wheat Sunday 25th I attended meeting br W.S. Snow & Peacock preached first rate to us Monday 26th Tuesday 27th Wednesday 28th I called out the Militia of Ephraim and inspected their arms & also organized the new comers Thursday 29th Friday 30th It stormed very hard & we turned out ennofs & fixed up the publick Correll

. . .

Saturday May 1st—I finished sowing wheat

Sunday 2nd—I attended meeting we had a good time

Monday 3rd—I sowed some flax & hemp

Tuesday 4th—I was in council with the Bishop

Wednesday 5th—I planted some garden seeds sutch as potatoes beets peas shugur cain & corn

Thursday 6th—I attended the fast meeting it stormed

Friday 7th—I called out the people to tranzact some publick business

Satturday 8th—we turned out ennnofs and worked on willow creek ditch

Sunday 9th—all well cold & clear I attended meeting Brothers Heywood & and Peacock preached to us

Monday 10th—I planted some shugar cain & corn

Tuesday 11th—I planted some beans & squashes

Wednesday 12th—I sowed 2 acres of oats

Thursday 13th—I planted some potatoes

Friday 14th—I finished putting in potatoes

Saturday 15th—I put in 2 acres more of oats

Sunday 16th—I attended meeting brs Wareham & Cox preached to us

Monday 17th—I went to Manti City on publick business

Tuesday 18th—I sowed some barley

Wednesday 19th—I went to Manti to see about the division of the herd ground

Thursday 20th—I went to the duck spring to meet my brother Isaac & in the after noon I held an officer drill

Friday 21st—I went south & got a load of saleratus it was tolerable good

Saturday 22nd—I assisted Brother Isaac to put in some flax seed

Sunday 23rd—I attended meeting brs Snow & Edwards gave us some good instructions

Monday 24th—I put in some potatoes for father

Tuesday 25th—I put in some peas & beans for father

Wednesday 26th—I had another Officer drill

Thursday 27th—I made myself a pair of mockinson

Friday 28th—I went to the mountains for saw logs

Friday 29th—I went to Manti with it

Sunday 30th—I attended meeting & while I was speaking there came an express to me from Manti to raise ten men to go south in persuit of some Indians that had stolen some horses & mules from beaver County & I immediately raised the men & started south through Manti & on south to salt creek & then southeast to the gunnison trail which is ninety or one hundred miles here we rested awhile & found that we had headed them it being Monday 31st we started back on the road and had not travelled far until we seen them comeing we therefore waited until came up with in about a mile and we then salied forth to try and surround them but quite a number of them made their escape we got 43 head of horses & mules they fired on us several times but only killed one of our mens horses we then started home and travelled 10 miles & camped

Tuesday June 1st 1858—we traveled about 40 miles & camped

Wednesday 2nd—we traveled 44 miles and arrived at home all well but very tired & sore by riding

Thursday 3rd—I attended fast meeting

Friday 4th—I made some oxboes and just at dusk news came that there was three men & one woman was killed in salt creek canion therefore I immediately raised 30 men & started after the dead bodies & we arrived at the place of masicree

Saturday 5th—just at day break we gathered up the dead bodies & returnd home they was Danish people that was killed one man only made his escape he was a sweed

Sunday 6th—all well I attended meeting

Monday 7th—I attended county court

Tuesday 8th Wednesday 9th Thursday 10th Friday 11th Saturday 12th—I was working on water ditches & damses

Sunday 13th—all well & fine weather I attended meeting

Monday 14th Tuesday 15—I worked on brother Isaac Allreds house

Wednesday 16th—I watered my Fathers garden lot & attended Officer drill

Thursday 17th—It rained quite a shower

Friday 18th—I went to the Mountains after coal

Saturday 19th—I halled a load of wood

Sunday 20th—I attended meeting all well

Monday 21st—I moved in to another house

Tuesday 22nd—I was fixing up about the house

Wednesday 23rd—all well & fine weather I attended Officer drill

Thursday 24th—I was quite unwell threw the days

Friday 25th—I pulled some flax

Saturday 26th—I attended quorum[11] meeting

Sunday 27th—I attended public meeting

Monday 28th—I gathered some more wild flax

Tuesday 29th—I went to the mountains to work on the road & get mill timber

Wednesday 30th—I had the bowery fixed up

Thursday July 1st 1858 Friday 2nd—I worked on a public back house

Saturday 3rd—we had a drill & inspection of arms & also some good beer

Sunday 4th—I attended meeting Presidents to Chapman Wareham & Cox spoke to us & gave us some good instructions

Monday 5th—all well fine weather

Tuesday 6th—I put some flax in lot and watered

Wednesday 7th—I pulled some more weeds

Thursday 8th—I went to the mountains

Friday 9th—I worked on br Clafsfes house

---

[11] General Assembly of the Mormon Priesthood

Saturday 10th—I halled stone for a meeting house

Sunday 11th—I attended meeting all well

Monday 12th—I put up some damaged adobies & worked on Madson water ditch

Tuesday 18th—I went up north to work on the road and returned home

Wednesday 14th—all well

Thursday 15th—I put in some turnips

Friday 16th—I halled some more stone for the meeting house on tithing

Saturday 17th—I went to the Mountains

Sunday 18th—all well fine weather I attended meeting Bishop Snow &council spoke

Monday 19th—I went to the mountain for timber

Tuesday 20th—I went a trip north to look for Indians

Wednesday 21st—halled stone for P.Burison

Thursday 22nd—I went to the mountains for logs

Friday 23rd—I went to Manti City

Saturday 24th—we celebrated this day it being the 11th anniversary of the entrance of the pioneers into Great Salt Lake Valley we had a first rate time

Sunday 25th—all well fine weather I attended meeting brother Wareham & Cox preached

Monday 26th—I went to the Mountains for logs

Tuesday 27th—I went to Manti with my logs

Wednesday 28th—I stacked up my lumber

Thursday 29th—I cut some wheat

Friday 30th—I burned some brush for ashes

Saturday 31st—I went to Manti to attend a convention

Sunday August 1st 1858—all well fine weather I attended meeting br Snow & Peacock preached

Monday 2nd—I helped to make a ford road a cross the creek on the County

Tuesday 3rd—I halled up my flax

Wednesday 4th—I halled a load of wood

Thursday 5th—I went to the mountains Ehmist

Friday 6th—I borrowed 7 bushels & 12 lbs of wheat of Thomas Thorpe & I had previously got 9 bushels & 7 lbs & I watered my turnip path

Saturday 7th—I cut some wheat

Sunday 8th—all excited about fine weather I attended meeting brothers Chapman Wareham& Cox preached

Monday 9th—I went to the mountains for ribs & slufsers

Tuesday 10th—I pulled my flax

Wednesday 11th—I went & got a load of posts

Thursday 12th—I commenced my shed

Friday 13th Saturday 14th—I was cutting wheat

Sunday 15th—two of the children quite unwell I attended meeting fine weather

Monday 16th—I finished my shed

Tuesday 17th—I halled a load of hay

Wednesday 18th—I started to salt creek canion after hops and Thursday 19th returned back home again traveled 60 miles

Friday 20th Saturday 21st—I was halling & putting up hay

Sunday 22nd—My first wife is quite unwell

Monday 23rd—I made me a rake & bound some wheat

Tuesday 24th—I halled a load of wheat

Wednesday 25th—my wife Eliza was so bad off that I stayed at home all day

Thursday 26th—she was a little better

Friday 27th Saturday 28th—I was halling & cutting hay

Sunday 29th—I went up north to look at the country

Monday 30th—my wife was worse again

Tuesday 31st—I halled wheat all day

Wednesday Sept 1st 1858—I halled a load of wood

Thursday 2nd Friday 3rd Saturday 4th—I was cutting putting up & halling hay

Sunday 5th—my wife is a little better

Monday 6th—it stormed all day

Tuesday 7th—I pulled up my peas

Wednesday 8th—my wife was taken worse again

Thursday 9th Friday 10th—I was cutting wheat my wife is still very bad off

Saturday 11th—my wife is very sick

Sunday 12th—my wife still very sick

Monday 13th—I harvested some wheat

Tuesday 14th—my wife still very bad off

Wednesday 15th—at home all day taking care of my wife who was very sick the old sow had eleven pigs

Thursday 16th—I was harvesting

Friday 17th Saturday 18th—I was harvesting

Sunday 19th—my wife is a litttle better

Monday 20th—I fix up my stock yard & thrashed some peas

Tuesday 21st—halled a load of hay

Wednesday 22nd—I halled a load of Tithing hay

Thursday 23rd—I halled aload of hay

Friday 24th—I halled some peas

Saturday 25th—I halled aload of hay

Sunday 26th—my wife is still favorly & my youngest child is very sick

Monday 27th—I finished halling hay

Tuesday 28th—I cut up my hemp & halled it

Wednesday 29th—I halled stone for the foundation of my house

Thursday 30th—I went to the mountains for poles

Friday Oct 1st 1858—I layed off the foundation of my house

Saturday 2nd—It rained & I attended my quorum meeting & my sick folks is better

Sunday 3rd—my second wife is very sick

Monday 4th—I layed the foundation to my house

Tuesday 5th—my second wife was delivered of an heir at 10 o clock it ill & we had it blessed & named it John Richard Allred it was blessd by its Grand Father Patriarch James Allred

Wednesday 6th—very stormy my folks is as well as could be expected except John Richard Allred who departed this life at about Elieves o clock

Thursday 7th—I intered my infant child clear day

Friday 8th—it stormed I laid some adobies on my house

Saturday 9th—I laid adobies

Sunday 10th—I attended meeting my wife is gaining a little

Monday 11th—I lay some potatoes

Tuesday 12th—I went to the mountains after polez

Wednesday 13th Thursday 14th Friday 15th—I was digging my potatoez & unions

Saturday 16th—It stormed all day the snow fell about 6 inches I attended my Quorum meeting

Sunday 17th—still storming my sick folks are better

Monday 18th—I worked on the road

Tuesday 19th—I finished digging potatoes

Wednesday 20th—I set up my wheat to dry

Thursday 21st Friday 22nd—I was halling & stacking my wheat

Saturday 23rd—I fixed up me a cow correll

Sunday 24th—I attended meeting

Monday 25th—I dug beets

Tuesday 26th—I started south on a mission to the Indians & I traveled threw Manti City and on to the Indian farm 19 miles

Wednesday 27th—I traveled south 30 miles

Thursday 28th—I traveled south 35 miles

Friday 29th—I traveled south 30 miles and arrived at the Arapenes camp in the sever valley I had quite a long talk with him he treated me very kindly & friendly

Saturday 30th—I started back home and traveled 35 miles

Sunday 31st—I traveled 60 miles

Monday November 1st 1858—I arrived at home traveled 19 mz

Tuesday 2nd—I cleaned up wheat

Wednesday 3rd—I halled some headings

Thursday 4th—my first wife Eliza was confined & she brought forth a son she had a very hard time

Friday 5th—I worked on my house

Saturday 6th—I layed adobies on my house

Monday 7th—my wife is very sick

Monday 8th Tuesday 9th—I layed adobies on my house

Wednesday 10th—I finished the adobie works on my house & put on the ribs

Thursday 11th—I went to the mountains for poles to cover my house

Friday 12th Saturday 13th—I was covering my house Saturday afternoon I attended my Quorum meeting

Sunday 14th—my wife is a little better & Patriarch James Allred blessed our youngest child & called his name William Hackley Allred

Monday 15th Tuesday 16th Wednesday 17th—I was working on my house

Thursday 18th—I went to Manti to Mill

Friday 19th—I was unwell

Saturday 20th—It stormed all day and I attended Philo Dibbles exibition of the marterdom of Joseph & Hyrum Smith the Martyred prophet & patriarch and I purchased a perpetual right to attend it for myself and my family by paying five dollars in wheat

Sunday 21st—my wife is gaining slowly it is a very cold day snow about 4 or 5 inches

Monday 22nd—I snowed considerable

Tuesday 23rd—was my wedding day

Wednesday 24th Thursday 25th Friday 26th Saturday 27th—I was working on my house

Sunday 28th—I attended meeting br Snow & Edwards spoke well to us

Monday 29th—I killed my pig it weighed 150 lbs 7 months old

Tuesday 30th—I was working on my house

Wednesday December 1st 1858 Thursday 2nd Friday 3rd Saturday 4th—I was working on my house laying floors

Sunday 5th—I attended meeting all well

Monday 6th Tuesday 7th Wednesday 8th Thursday 9th Friday 10th Saturday 11th—I was plastering and finishing off the inside of my house and I was all most blind with the sore eyes

Sunday 12th—my eyes was very bad

Monday 13th—my eyes are a little better

Tuesday 14th—I had my wheat & oats cleaned

Wednesday 15th—I put my wheat into my new house

Thursday 16th—I moved my family in to my new house it was very cold weather

Friday 17th Saturday 18th—I was fixing up about my house and yard

Sunday 19th—cold & clear attended meeting brs Champan Wareham & Cox preached to us first rate

Monday 20th—I halled some straw

Tuesday 21st Wednesday 22nd—I was performing a mifsion that bishop Snow & Peacock gave me to perform

Thursday 23rd Friday 24th—I was Tinkering about home

Saturday 25th—clear & cold we had a very dull Christmas

Sunday 26th—all well clear & cold

Monday 27th Tuesday 28th Wednesday 29th Thursday 30th Friday 31st—I was meeting in private council with my brethren boath here & at Manti City & also watc ing around to help to feri out iniquity from within the midst of the saints in Fort Ephraim There are some individuals that are trying to pull down the Bishop & his council in Fort Ephraim & also in Manti City namely Benjamin T. Clapp & Tory Thurston & others

Saturday January 1st 1859—cold & clear I went to Manti & met in the high council & the case of BT Clapp & Thurston & others was take in to consideration & it was a unanimous vote of the council that they be cut from the church of Jesus Christ of Latter Day Saints

Sunday 2nd—I attended Conference in Manti and the above named individuals with several others was cut off from the church

Monday 3rd—at home cold & clear

Tuesday 4th—early in the morning The Bishop called the people together to let some of the brethren make a confefsion that had been cut off whitch they done & it was a unanimous vote of the people to forgive them & that they have the priveledge of coming back into the church at the door in the afternoon brother Chapman Wareham & Cox & Edwards preached to us on the principle of takeing care of our wheat & also on many other good principle

Wednesday 5th—cold & clear

Thursday 6th—I attended fast meeting

Friday 7th Saturday 8th—very cold & clear at home

Sunday 9th—I attended meeting

Monday 10th Tuesday 11th Wednesday 12th Thursday 13th—about home the most of my time I was walking around and this evening brothers E.J. Benson & E Snow arrived in Ephraim & we met in council

Friday 14th—They held a publick meeting their instructions was good

Saturday 15th—I went to Manti to a two days meeting in the evening I attended a council and it was taken into consideration what to do for Ephraim wheather to organize it over or not it waz not concluded upon what would be done

Sunday 16th—we had good instructions by the apostles in the evening I attended the church meeting

Monday 17th—I returned home & When I arrived I found that my Indian boy had stolen my bro Reubens horse and ran away & Reuben followed him in the evening I attend meeting & after wards council and in the council Ephraim was disorganized & CG. Edwards was chozen to act as our future Bishop & President Protem

Tuesday 18th—I attended meeting we had good instructions in the after noon bro Reuben arrived home with my boy he got him at Nephi City

Wednesday 19th—we had a Priest hood meeting and P.E. Koffod res sined his office & C. G. Edwardz was unanimously sustained by vote to be President for the time being

Thursday 20th—the apostles left us and started home during thier stay I baptized Eleven of the Brethren that had been cut off

Friday 21st—at home cold & clear

Saturday 22nd—I had a supper made for my Father it being his seventy fifth birthday

Sunday 23rd—I attended meeting

Monday 24th Tuesday 25th Wednesday 26th Thursday 27th Friday 28th Saturday 29th—I was watching & teaching others most all the time

Sunday 30th—I attended meeting

Monday 31st—I was watching around

Tuesday Feb 1st 1859 Wednesday 2nd Thursday 3rd—I was all so watching

Friday 4th Saturday 5th—I halled two loads of Oak & cotton wood for to make ashes for soap

Sunday 6th—I attended meeting brothers Chapman Wareham & Cox preached to us & gave us good instructions

Monday 7th Tuesday 8th—I was halling firewood for myself

Wednesday 9th—I was on gard

Thursday 10th Friday 11th—I went up north after hardwood for plow stocks & co—

Saturday 12th—I was on gard

Sunday 13th—I attended meeting

Monday 14th—I halled a load of wood

Tuesday 15th Wednesday 16th—I was on gard

Thursday 17th—I halled a load of wood

Friday 18th—it stormed I was on gard

Saturday 19th—I halled a load of wood

Sunday 20th—clear & cold all well I attended meeting we had a good time

Monday 21st—I halled a load of wood

Tuesday 22nd—I thashed some oats & barley

Wednesday 23rd—I was on guard

Thursday 24th—I was on guard

Friday 25th—I went to Manti

Saturday 26th—I was watching around

Sunday 27th—clear& calm I attended meeting brothers Wareham & Snow spoke

Monday 28th—I halled a load of wood

Tuesday March 1st 1859—I cleaned up some Oats & barley

Wednesday 2nd—I was on guard

Thursday 3rd—I attended meeting

Friday 4th—I was on guard

Saturday 5th—I halled a load of wood

Sunday 6th—I attended meeting

Monday 7th—I went to Manti City to attend the County Court

Tuesday 8th—I returned home

Wednesday 9th Thursday 10th Friday 11th Saturday 12th—I was halling wood for myself

Sunday 13th—cold & clear this night my Indian boy ran away with the soldiers

Monday 14th Tuesday 15th Wednesday 16th Thursday 17th Friday 18th Saturday 19th—I was on guard the most of the time

Sunday 20th—I attended meeting

Monday 21st Tuesday 22 Wednesday 23rd Thursday 24th Friday 25th Saturday 26th—I was engaged considerable of my time on the bridge & tithing meeting house & also on guard watching for our enemy

Sunday 27th—I attended meeting

Monday 28th Tuesday 29th Wednesday 30 Thursday 31st Friday April 1st 1859 Saturday 2nd—I was attending to public bufsinefs

Sunday 3rd—I attended meeting

Monday 4th Tuesday 5th Wednesday 6th Thursday 7th Friday 8th Saturday 9th—I was on guard & other publick work

Saturday 9th—I started my plow

Sunday 10th—I attended meeting & in the afternoon some U.S. soldiers & a debtey Marshall arrived here & was after some of the brethren I went to Manti City

Monday 11th—I returned home

Tuesday 12th Wednesday 13th Thursday 14th Friday 15th Saturday 16th—I was plowing & sowing wheat & grubbing

Sunday 17th—I attended meeting & br Caleb G. Edwards chose Christian Christianson to be his first councillor & myself to be the second

Monday 18th Tuesday 19th—I was grubing my land

Wednesday 20th Thursday 21st Friday 22nd—I was scouting around the country

Saturday 23rd—I sowed & harrowed some wheat

Sunday 24th—I attended meeting

Monday 25th Tuesday 26th Wednesday 27th—I was putting in wheat & grubbing

Thursday 28th—I went to Manti City

Friday 29th—I went to the west mountains on an exploring expedition and I was searching out the facilities of the country until Friday May 20th 1859 I returned home again and found all well

Saturday 21st—I went up willow creek canion & shot an old grisily bear but did not get it

Sunday 22nd—I attended meeting

Monday 23rd Tuesday 24th Wednesday 25th Thursday 26th Friday 27th Saturday 28th—I was working on water ditches all the week myself & team & another hand the most of the time

Sunday 29th—I was watering my wheat to make it come up

Monday 30th—I was watering

Tuesday 31st—I was plowing some land for to sow some oats & peas

Wednesday June 1st 1859 Thursday 2nd Friday 3rd Saturday 4th—I was plowing & sowing & watering oats peas all the week

Sunday 5th—I was watering

Monday 6th—I went to Manti City to attend county Court

Tuesday 7th—I hired Jens Monson for six months if he suits me & him and I am to give him 35 bus of wheat & 15 bushels of corn if he stays with me six months & works well & co

Wednesday 8th—I was watering

Thursday 9th—I was putting up fence

Friday 10th—I was working on the road

Saturday 11th—I put up some more fence

Sunday 12th—I attended meeting all well

Monday 13th—I was irrigating my wheat

Tuesday 14th—I went to Manti City

Wednesday 15th Thursday 16th Friday 17th Saturday 18th—I was halling poles

Sunday 19th—I was watering wheat

Monday 20th—I sowed some turnips

Tuesday 21st Wednesday 22nd—I was halling poles

Thursday 23rd—I halled a load of posts

Friday 24th—I fixed up a shade

Saturday 25th—I halled a load of timber

Sunday 26th—warmer & cloudy all well attended meeting

Monday 27th Tuesday 28th Wednesday 29th—I was putting up an ox frame for Br Edminton to shoe my oxen

Thursday 30th—I was hunting some tar wood & red pine for to peal some torn beark

Friday July 1st 1859 Saturday 2nd—I was watering wheat & oats

Sunday 3rd—I attended meeting

Monday 4th—I attended a publick dinner made by the Quire

Tuesday 5th—I got my oxen shod

Wednesday 6th—I was watering

Thursday 7th—I attended fast meeting

Friday 8th—It rained and showered

Saturday 9th—I halled a load of wood

Sunday 10th—I went to Mount Pleasant along with brother Smith & Lyman & heard them preach & they organized that place by putting Wm Sesly Presiding Bishop

Monday 11th—I returned home & heard them preach to the people of Ephraim

Tuesday 12th—I went to Manti City & attended meeting they spoke well to the people their

Wednesday 13th Thursday 14th Friday 15th Saturday 16th—I was halling poles

Sunday 17th—I attended meeting

Monday 18th Tuesday 19th—I was working tithing on the mountains

Wednesday 20th—I halled a load of poles for Jas ef Leemonz

Thursday 21st—I made a swing

Friday 22nd—I made some posts

Saturday 23rd—we celebrated with a dance & songs & speaches

Sunday 24th—I attended meeting

Monday 25th Tuesday 26th—I went to the Mountains for poles

Wednesday 27th Thursday 28th Friday 29th Saturday 30th—I was getting posts & putting up a stock yard & correll

Sunday 31st—I attended meeting

7

JAMES T.S. ALLRED ARRIVED IN EPHRAIM November 26, 1855. While home, he took a second wife, the widowed sister of his wife, Margaret Mainwaring Roberts. Sometime after April 19, 1856, James T.S. Allred and his families returned to Las Vegas, Nevada, arriving May 29, 1856. They settle into life once again building up a community. Edward Francis Allred is born September 5, 1856 to James T.S. and Eliza Allred. On February 11, 1857, Sarah Ann Allred is born to James T.S. and Margaret Allred. Brigham Young ordered all missionaries to return to Utah in 1857. Allred and his families returned safely to Ephraim on March 18, 1857, where they spend the next five years.

His oldest daughter, Eliza Maria, wrote her account of life in Ephraim:

> We resided in Ephraim several years. My father was gone most of the time laboring among the Indians. At this time they would get very hostile and angry. At one time they came and surrounded my father's house to kill us. My father told me to go and give the alarm He said, "If I go they will shoot me at my appearance." He thought if they saw a little child it might soften their hearts, so he said, "When you go I will get my weapons and come out." When I went to the door the Indians dropped off their horses and my father came out saying in their own language, "Shoot, but remember I have brothers and friends that will revenge my blood." They got in a circle and smoked the pipe of peace.

> My father was gone a great deal of the time among the Indians he being an Indian interpreter. He would tell me to keep plenty of bullets ready to supply both the Indians and the militia. The Indians would come and trade their goods for ammunition. At that time father was a captain over the militia.

The second eldest daughter, Ellen Aurelia Allred Nielsen, wrote of the family's years spent in Ephraim:

> My father was a hard worker and planner and a good provider, and so good and kind to my mother. That terrible fear of the Indians never left my mother, she had a constant dread of the Indians and my fathers contact with them. Pres. Young made many requests for father to make visits to the Indian camps to talk with them. Pioneer life was very hard, clothing was so costly and shoes cost so much you could only afford to wear them in cold weather. At school I had a Bible, Book of Mormon and a Blue back spelling book, and I had to set on an old rough slab, without a back rest, it is funny that I learned as much as I did. But I had lots of nice friends, both boys and girls. At night we had to study by the light of a rag in a platter of grease. Later we learned how to make candles, which was a pleasant improvement. At Christmas time we made rag dolls and carved things out of wood and gave a roasted potato and some home made candy. We surely had some lovely parties and we had lots of good sleigh rides, and at our parties no gambling cards was allowed, fruit basket was enjoyed very much, and of course a party was never a success unless you had a game of post office, it was quiet an exciting game.

Peaceful days of family life, and the start of her romance with Mads Neilsen, are described by Ellen:

> Lots of fun awaited us when the Indians were more peaceable and father and other Pioneers moved back to Spring City. Then lots of new people were coming from the old country, England and Denmark and other places. I remember when the Neils Nielsen family come to Sanpete County, they were surely lovely people. I said to my mother, that Mads Nielsen is sure a nice fellow, and he can speak pretty good english and he is sure nice to me, as he speak to me every time he sees me. My mother said I agree with you, he is a fine young man but he is much to old for you, so let him prectice his english on some one his own age. So in a few days we heard that they were going to Circleville, out in Piute County, and I fell quiet bad, but I didn't say anything to anybody. Mother sent me on an errand a few blocks away from home and when I was returning some one on a horse rode up to the side of me and said hello Ellen, and stopped and it was Mads, I was sure glad to see him, and he said that he was on his way to say good bye to me, so I Am so glad that I found you. Now Ellen I know how your parents feel about me, and I don't want you to worry, for I believe that things will turn out right for us. so I think very much of you and I hope that you like me just a little, I don't want to frighten you so good bye and remember how I feel toward you until I see you again, and he patted my head and rode away. And I didn't see him for many months. My father said at the supper table, that Mads was going to drive team for some freight out fit.

While living in Ephraim, John Richard Allred was born October 5, 1858 to James T.S. and Margaret Allred. As noted in Allred's

Daybook, he died the next day. On February 14, 1860, Barbara Allred was born to Fanny Shantaquint and James T.S. Allred. Fanny Shantaquint and James T.S. Allred had been married in 1858 and sealed December 13, 1862.

Fanny Shantaquint Allred, a member of the Ute Indian Tribe, was born on March 4, 1842, in Utah County, Utah. The Utes or Nuche—"The People"—inhabited the flatlands of central Utah to the western Rocky Mountains. They lived in independent bands or families often named for the area they occupied, but would travel long distances for gatherings. The size of these bands and the area through which they migrated depended primarily on the availability of natural resources. The Mormon's encroachment on Native American lands united the various indigenous people.

Fanny Shanataquint was most likely a member of the Tumpanawach or Timpanogos, who lived near Utah Lake, or the San Pete, San Pitch or Sanpits, who occupied Sanpete County and Sevier County. The Tumpanawach were a large, powerful and more mobile band having access to permanent food resources. The San Pete of Sanpete County had limited resources. Early pioneers described their poor living conditions.

James T. S. Allred writes in April 1856:

> Wednesday 16th I traveled to Springville Thursday 17th I traded my horse and mule for two yoke of oxen and traveled to the shonte quint springs 15 miles

Fanny Shantaquint's last name resembles that of Ute Chief Santaquin who resided near the southeastern shore of Utah Lake and for whom the town of Santaquin was named in 1857. It is near where Chief Antonga Black Hawk was born and died. It is possible this was her birthplace and where she met Allred given the topography, the migration routes and historical interaction with early Mormon settlers.

Her birth date is given as 1842—before the introduction of horses by pioneers to the San Pete. It is therefore more likely she was a member of the San Pete and travelled to Ephraim where in 1857 she was sold, traded, or met Allred. Few facts are known about this seminal figure. Her life remains a whisper throughout this narrative.

8

THE VALLEY FORMS A CIRCLE.

Circle Valley had been a hunting ground for the Native Americans. Numerous arrowheads were at one time found in the canyons. Rock carvings of men, deer, snakes, trees, send silent messages to the spirits.

James T.S. Allred first came to Circle Valley in December of 1863. Allred, his brother Andrew Jackson Allred, his son-in-law, James Munson, as well as four others from Ephraim, Utah, came to explore the possibility of establishing a settlement in Circle Valley, along the Sevier River.

In 1849, an expedition led by Parley Pratt had followed the Sevier River through the Circle Valley and found the undergrowth so thick it was impossible for travel on horseback. The expedition turned west into the Parowan Valley. The Sevier River is named either for the Paiute word for mammoth, *sevee u*, a picture of which is depicted in nearby petroglyphs; or for the Spanish name Rio Severo (River Severe), in honor of the turbulent and unpredictable nature of the river especially in the spring.

Between the Parowan Valley and the Circle Valley rise the Tushar Mountains with Delano Peak rising to 12,173 feet and to the north, Mount Baldy rising to 12,008 feet and Mount Belknap rising to 12,139 feet. Southeast, Circleville Mountain rises to 11,440 feet. The mountains are capped with snow most years providing ample water for the valley. Cottonwood Creek runs into the Sevier River south of the town of Circleville. Birch Creek flows down the south slopes of Circleville Mountain joining the Sevier River and Cottonwood Creek. It is here they merge with the East Fork of the Sevier River. The valley formed by the Sevier River and the East Fork of the Sevier is about ten miles wide. On the east rises the Sevier Plateau. Mount Dutton, southwest of Circleville is 10,800 feet high. The plateau on the east ranges from 7500 feet to 9500 feet high.

The Sevier River ambles north through the valley meandering through marshlands and cutting through brightly colored rock that in springtime washes into the river turning the river mustard yellow for miles. In summer, it could easily be crossed, but in spring it would prove dangerous. A snowstorm in June is not unusual. The land west over the mountain passes resembles the Great Basin. The Old Spanish Trail runs along Bear Creek and Little Creek and was used by the Spaniards and Indians as trade routes. Circleville is located on The Old Spanish Trail. The Paiute Indians were often captured and sold into slavery by their cousins, the Ute Indians as well as the Spaniards.

The clouds are grey blue in spring. There is a mist hovering in the air softening the spring pinks, light greens and yellows. The summer fields are irrigated from melting snow flowing from the mountains. Sagebrush covers the hillsides. As the season turns to autumn, the mountains are scattered with gold from the patches of white barked aspen. Their trunks dance an old man dance in the mountains from where they have borne the winter snow. The cottonwood and poplar trees shake off their leaves in the wind dance and the silhouettes scatter throughout the valley where once a farmhouse rested.

South of Circleville, where the valley opens into soft pastureland, stands Bear Valley Junction located at the junction of Bear Creek and the Sevier River. This is where Fort Sanford used to stand. North of Circleville is Marysvale, another sleepy town along the Sevier River. Circleville, Fort Sanford and Marysvale were the only towns located in this valley in the 1860s isolated between the Tushar Mountains on the west and the Sevier Plateau on the east. At its widest, the valley is six miles wide. It was fifteen miles between Circleville and where Fort

Sanford stood. It is twenty miles between Circleville and Marysvale. It was an isolated and inaccessible location.

In 1864 Brigham Young called on fifty families to move to the valley:

> Col. Wm. H. Dame, G.S.L. March 14, 1864
>
> It will therefore be the commencement of a permanent settlement. Nearly all attempts at building Forts in the Ter.T of Utah have proved failures, and if a company of men go over to the head of the Sevier, it will only be necessary to lay out a village, so that each man can occupy a lot, and according to the nature of the ground from ¾ to 1 ¼ acres, not allowing men to take more than one or at least for the present and this according to the Council given to C.C. Rich and those who are living in Richland Co. so that if a woman should scream from the intrusion of a villain, white, black, or red, that the neighbor would be likely to hear. The President is unwilling to give his consent that men should settle their families promiscuously knowing the wiles of the Devil, red, black and white. I therefore counsel the brethren to locate in a village and not to spread their houses so far apart that they will not afford from their proximity ample protection to each other, and where buildings are actually built on lots where men expect to remain, they will plant out fruit trees, and make other arrangements, which are of great value in the early attainment of domestic fruits, shades and other necessaries.
>
> I do not think it would be hardly proper for you to permanently leave Parowan without the direction of the President until other directions are given.
>
> I am very respectfully
> Your Brother
> Geo.A. Smith

> I have read this to Pres. Young and he remarked I wish they had it now to act on it.

These fifty families from Sanpete County arrived on March 28, 1864, and lived in dugouts. Soon after they arrived, the town and the surrounding farmland were surveyed and each family drew lots for a town plot and ten acres of farmland. They settled on both sides of the river but the best farmland was on the east side of the river. By June 12, 1865, one hundred families inhabited Circleville.

On February 18, 1865, correspondent and Paiute County Judge Edward Tolton from Circleville wrote to the *Deseret News* that four miles of canal had been built and ten miles of canyon roads had been completed. They opened the road between Circleville and Beaver and Parowan on the west side of the Tushar Mountains. He wrote:

> At present the road is barely passable and will require considerable more labor to make it easy for teams, but we are sure of seeing these obstacles removed, and a great thoroughfare to the South running along this route into Dixie, at no distant day. Several substantial homes are now completed including our meeting house, and we are now engaged in uniting our efforts to establish a school. Mr. William M. Black is making preparations to erect a good grist mill and Mr. John Reynolds intends to build a good sawmill as soon as practicable. With these desirable facilities our progress will be more rapid. These people are fully determined to demonstrate that they will attend to their own business, honor their mission and make this place a desirable location for the Saints.

Digging irrigation ditches began at once. Gophers burrowed in the canals causing many of the ditches to leak. By the spring of 1865, an irrigation ditch on the west side of the Sevier six feet wide and thirty inches deep watered about four hundred acres, not including the hay land. By June, on the east side of the Sevier, an upper ditch watered three hundred acres. Other irrigation ditches were located on the west side of the river and one from the East Fork of the Sevier.

James T.S. Allred and his son-in-law James Munson cut and hauled the logs from Cottonwood Canyon used to build the first log house in Circleville where church meetings were held. William J. Allred, a second cousin of James T.S. Allred's, was appointed Mormon bishop. James T.S. Allred was Captain of the town militia.

Most settlers had built homes by the fall of 1865, which protected them from the severe winds. Many settlers became discouraged and left the settlement. Others came to join the Circleville residents so the settlement maintained a population of about forty families. On October 24, 1865, the newspaper correspondent Edward Tolton wrote, "Though surrounded by Indians they have so far had no difficulty with them."

*

James T.S. Allred and his family moved to Circleville Utah in March 1864. Daily life in Circleville is best described by Ellen Aurelia Allred, when her future husband Mads Neilsen and others are courting her:

> There was another young man who was very nice to me but my father said he wasn't worth his salt and he didn't want him hanging around us girls. Mother used to say to father, now my dear these girls of ours, should have a boy friend once in a while. And he would reply, I know that, but I don't like a lazy cuss hanging around, I would rather have an old maid on my hands, than one of them good for nothings.
>
> I had another problem as there were two married men, with two wives each, and four kids each and both of them were all smiles when they met me, either in church or the street. And I was afraid that they might get it in their noggins

that Ellen Allred would make a good third wife. So one evening we were finishing our supper, when mother said we are going to have company, so in a few minutes a tap come on the door, and when mother opened the door there stood brother so and so, with his two wives, and mother invited them in, and told them to make them selves at home. I knew in a minute that I was in for trouble, for this was one of the men that I mentioned before that had tried to be nice to me, and I had avoided him for weeks. So Father broke the silence, by saying it is surely nice to have you folks come to see us. And the visitor replied Brother Allred, me and my wives have come to ask you and sister Allred for your daughter Ellen, we have made it a matter of prayer and we feel that the Lord has answered our prayers, and that is why we are here tonight. My mother was helping me with the dishes, and when the man mentioned my name she dropped a large plate on the floor. Then father seeing how upset mother was, he motioned for her to come over to him and set down. My face was so red and I was so embarrassed, I left the room and closed the door behind me.

And then my sister Dianthia come to my rescue an we stood by the door and listened. My father sat a few minutes in deep silence, and then he replied, now my dear brother, me and my dear wife appreciate you folks coming, and we feel honored to have you request our daughter Ellen for your third wife. But we have other plans for our daughter, we feel she should have a right to choose a sweet heart of her own, for she is a beautiful girl and we love her very much. Now if my dear wife don't have anything further to say, we will bid you good night. And they got up and left. And when I opened the door, my dear mother come and took me in her arms and we had a good cry.

Then my father, said to mother, that is a lesson for me, I want you to have some very nice parties here at home, and invite the best boys and girls in our town to come. We want our daughters and sons to get acquainted with the best we can find. And we had a lot of marvelous parties and father and mother helped us have a good time. The very next day I saw a man on a horse coming up the street, and turn at our corner, and get off his horse and it to the fence post. And when he opened the little gate and looked up

I was so surprised, it was Mads Nielsen, I hadn't seen him for him several months and he come and took my hands in his and said how glad he was to see me, and he said you are much prettier than when I saw you the last time. Now Ellen I have some thing very special to say to you today, but I must speak to your father and mother first.

We were standing right in front of the house and I know that mother and some of the kids were watching every thing that went on. He said Ellen I have told you several times how much I thought of you, and your father told me a long time ago, when we moved to Circleville that I was too old for you, and for me to wait and give you a chance to make up your own mind. Now Ellen my Dearest, I must ask you a question that means so much to me. Do you like me as much now as you did before I went away? And I thrilled all over when I answered. I care for you much more than you know, and I got the surprise of my life as he put his arms around me and gave me my first hug and kiss. I guess my mother thought it was time for her to open the door and invite us in side. I was so proud of him, and mother made a big fuss over him to and that pleased me a lot. In a little while we heard father drive into the yard and when he come into the house, mother said, my Dear, look who has come to see us. And father said what a pleasant surprise, Mads my boy I am sure glad to see you and how are your folks and you are looking in fine shape yourself. It made me feel so good to have my parents treat him so nice. When every one had found a place to set, father said now Mads what can we do to help you with, Mads put his chair right in front of my parents and set down, now Brother and sister Allred, this may be a big surprise for you both, and it may be one for Ellen also. But I love your daughter very much and I know that I Am older than she is, and since I have been away I have been planning for her to be my wife. I have worked very hard and now I have a good team and wagon and 5 head of cattle all paid for, and I have a log cabin about half built, and 20 acres of land partly paid for. And now I Am asking you as her parents, if you will consent for her to marry me? My mother was wiping the tears out of her eyes, and father looked straight at me, when he quietly said, well my boy that was very well said, mother and I think you are a fine young man and we feel very much honored to have you ask us for our daughter. Now don't you think it would be well and very much in order, to hear how Ellen feels about this affair. And Mads gave me another surprise as he come over to my chair and put one knee on the floor, and said Ellen my Dearest will you marry me, I love you very much and I will protect you with my life and I will work hard to make a home for you. He had his arm around me and I was half frightened, when I looked up and we were alone in the room as the folks had quietly slipped out and left us alone in the room, I had the most wonderful feeling as I put my arms around him, and told him how much I loved him, and the many times I had longed for him to return to me. He drew me very close and kissed me several times, and then said you better have your folks come back in.

So when the folks come back in the room and sat down, my mother asked me to come to her, and as I knelt by her side, she whispered in my ear, my Dear, I Am very proud of you. So father was the first one to speak, when he said, well my boy what did Ell have to say about your plans? And Mads replied Brother Allred let Ellen tell you, and when father looked at me I was crying so much that I couldn't speak a word, ther had be so many unexpected things happen in the last few hours, that it seemed that my entire life had changed in that time, and yet I was thrilling with happiness.

So father turned to my mother and asked her how she felt about her new son? My Dear mother held out her hand and told Mads to come to her, and she put her arms arund him, and told him how proud she was to let him marry her daughter, and then she kissed him. I knew that he was very tender hearted, and very affectionate, he put his head on my mothers lap and sobbed and cried for several minutes. No one spoke a single word, till my father had dried his own eyes, then he moved his chair over by mother and Mads, then he told me to come closer with my chair. Then he took Mads by the hand and told him how proud he was of him, and he said that good cry you just had made you a big man in my eyes. Now mother and I have a few more things to talk over with you two. We expect our children to go through the Endowment House as the Temple isn't completed yet. We want you to have your prayers, and pay your tithing and attend to all of your church duties at all times, and then you can expect the Lord to Bless you. So we planned for our wedding, to be held in about three weeks, and we had a lovely wedding and got lots of useful things and they were surely appreciated …

Ellen Aurelia Allred Neilsen continues her narrative, detailing events that unnerved the settlers of Circleville setting the stage for future acts of revenge.

> … We are going to make our home in Circleville. Well the wedding is over with and Mads is surely working hard to complete our little log cabin. He is so happy and he sings and whistles all the time, and I Am so happy. My older sister Eliza lives here in Circleville, she married James Munson, and they sure treat us good. My husband is sure my ideal and I love and appreciate him more each day, he is so kind and thoughtful of me. It surely a hot summer and harvest time has arrived. we sure had a good crop of wheat, and my Dear is so happy over every thing. He waits on me and helps me with everything. And in the near future we are going to go to Salt Lake City, and take a load of wheat, to buy our supplies for the winter. And several other people are going with us. We finally arrived in Salt Lake City, and it is sure a large place.
>
> My husband has done very well with our load of wheat, and we have bought so many nice things for our little home. And my husband has bought himself a new rifle and lots of ammunition, and is he happy over his new gun. Now my dear I can protect you for sure. Our trip from Salt Lake City, to Sanpete County, was uneventful no excitement out side of a lot of travelers, teams of oxen and teams of horses, and a few large freight wagons, and lots of dust. And some of these teamsters were awaful men to swear and cuss. We are leaving Ephraim this morning and it is very cold and frosty. There are several outfits traveling with us, as far as Richfield and that locality and my husband said we would be short of company after we left Marysvale. We arrived in Marysvale tonight and it is quiet late, and awful cold and out team is

very tired. It took us a full day to come over Monroe Mountain. There are three outfits here in camp tonight, and my dear man is so worried for he has just discovered that he left his new Rifle in Ephraim, and the only weapon he has for our protection is that broken pistol.

We are leaving Marysvale this morning, and my husband seems so worried, as a man with some cattle just joined us this morning. And my husband said he was afraid the cattle would make so much dust that the Indians would notice it and come after us, Now I Am going to relate something that I promised my beloved husband that I would never tell for three straight nights I awakened my husband, and told him of the dream that had just woke me up. In the dream I saw a herd of cattle being driven by a group of Indians and one Indian was on a white horse, and when the Indians saw our wagon they left the cattle and chased us, and when I screamed in my dream it awakened me and my husband also I have lived in fear for three days, and I know he is so worried, because in our prayers this morning he pleaded with the Lord to protect us one more day. All this forenoon my husband has urged the team and they are getting very tired. The other teams were loaded light and they have left us behind, andwe just saw my sister and her husband, and they said you will soon be home. The man with the cattle is quiet a ways back of us, and as we come around a little bend in the road, I looked across the river and saw a herd of cattle driven by a group of Indians, and there was the Indian on the white horse, and I screamed to my husband, there is my dream, please turn back, but he said my Dear our only chance is to make the point of the hill or that swamp. So you get back in the wagon and find the pistol. Then he whipped up the team and when the Indians saw us they left the cattle and come yelling after runing the team, and one Indian rode up to the side of the wagon and pointed his gun at my husband, and Mads pointed the pistol at him, then he turned and shot one of our horses. Then the Indians rode off to one side and my husband told me to get out of the wagon and take the baby and get in the swamp and willows, and he said I will come to protect you. As soon as I can. When I jumped in to the deep water up to my shoulders, I had to hold the boy out of the cold water for he would cry, he was so cold and I was so frightened, but I had my mind made up to drown myself and baby before I would let them savages get us. They set the wagon and things on fire, and then I was sure they had killed my husband, when an Indian come riding his horse in to the swamp and saw me and the baby, and just then my husband stood and pointed the pistol at him and he turned his horse around and got out of the swamp. My husband come and took the baby and got out of the swamp. My husband come and took the baby and got a hold of my arm, and said come my sweet heart that Redskin has gone for help, and I must get you to that bunch of bull rushes before they return. We had just made it to the rushes when we heard them over where the Indian had seen us. Finally the yelling stopped and I whispered to my husband, that they were leaving and he shook his head and held a finger in front of his mouth, and I knew that the savages were still around. It was getting dark and the light from our burning wagon was making the swamp so light we didn't dare to move very much, and we found out later that Froid[12] the man with the cattle, had been killed. My sister and her husband come by and saw our dead horse and burned wagon, and we could hear her crying, but my husband said there are four people over by that fire, so we thought the Indians had captured my sister and her husband. After they

[12] Floyd.

left we got out of the marsh and staid out of the road, until we got around the hill. It was so cold and our clothess were frozen stiff on us. We had been in the swamp since two o clock in the afternoon. My sister and her husband had just got in to town and reported what they had seen, so it was sure a surprise when we walked in, and they all treated us so good. And we were so thankful that our lives had been spared. Mads and several of the men went out to our wagon to see if they could find anything. Everything had been destroyed but one large platter and it had fell in the sand and was not broken. When my Dear Husband got back we set in our little log home with out anything, we were broke our team and wagon and four of our cattle and all of our supplies were gone, my darling husband took me in his arms and we had a good cry. Then we knelt down by our bed and thanked our Father in Heaven that he spared our lives. My husband said to me, now my Dearest I want you to make me a promise to never tell about your dream those three nights, for I feel so heart broken that I didn't take the warning that the Lord was trying to tell me to take you back to Ephraim away from all this danger. This all come to me as I stood guard over you and the baby back there in that swamp, with a broken pistol. Oh I feel that I have failed in protecting you, and what will your father think when he hears how I come very near of getting you killed. So the first opportunity I get in the next few months, I am getting you back up in Sanpete County, so it wasn't very many months after that, when the people had to leave Circleville for a while.

Now my beloved relatives and friends here in our little settlement of Circleville that means so much to me and you, I want you to know how much I appreciate the honor that you have showed me today, and may the Lord bless you all for it, so many thanks for everything.

Ellen Aurelia Allred Nielsen was sixty-nine years old when the above was written by her daughter in 1919 at a reunion in Marysvale. Ellen Aurelia Allred Nielsen died August 29, 1929 in Spring City, Utah.

The community had settled into a somewhat peaceful routine by the start of 1865. The settlers did take the precaution of standing guard day and night as hostile encounters between whites and Indians had taken place in Sanpete and Sevier Counties. Paiute County had so far been spared any hostile engagements in the Black Hawk War.

Eliza Marie Allred Munson penned the following song for the July 4th, 1864 celebration:

The command was given in 1864
The banks of the river in the South to explore
The teams were hitched up and rolled over the plain
But oh and alas they returned home again

Some did not like the country they said it was small
Some said very little some nothing at all
Some said of the country they could not complain
But alone in that country they dare not remain

The word was then given that they had to go
To settle that river above or below
The first ones that started from Ephraim fine town
Were Edward Tolton, James Munson, myself and Ashdown

We traveled along till we came to the cove
Where the water in the river was not very low
And the banks of the crossing were straight up and down
And the boys wished themselves in their own native town

We traveled and explored the country all round
But a good place to settle could not be found

Till we came to City Creek and made a short stand
To wait for the captain to give his command

We explored all next day and returned late at night
We had found water too scarce to make a townsite
So we hitched up in the morning and rolled on again
Wending our way over hill and plain

We traveled that day and the wind it did blow
The sand it flew thicker and faster than snow
I am sure it was mournful to hear the boys cry
Some said "I am blinded, Oh dear, my poor eyes"

At last we arrived and camped on the ground
Where the fine lofty mountains were circled all round
Except one small opening which some men did find
When they got discontented and altered their minds

Circle Valley is handsome although the winds blow
On the banks of the river the green bushes grow
There's a stream from the mountain like a bright silver chain
My home's in Circle Valley and there I'll remain

I hope we'll have union and peace in our town
Here's health to our captain and the boys all around

The hope for union and peace began to change on November 26, 1865. James T.S. Allred's two daughters, Eliza Marie Allred Munson and Ellen Aurelia Allred Nielsen, their husbands James Munson and Mads Nielsen, his three year old son, Brigham Young Allred as well as James Froid and Hans Christian Hansen were returning from Great Salt Lake City after getting provisions when they were attacked by a band of twelve Indians being led by Tamaritz, one of Ute Black Hawk's rising chiefs. Ellen's account is already given; Eliza Marie Allred Munson later wrote of the event:

> My father James T. S. Allred being an Indian interpreter engaged in many of the batles and was present when they smoked the pipe of peace. I was a witness to many Indian depredations in the Walker War and many others before the Black Hawk War.
>
> I personally knew him (Black Hawk) from the time he was 10 or 11 years of age. He was of the tribe of the low San Piches and was raised in Sanpete County. I should judge he was about 18 or 19 when he started his first depredations. He used to come to my father's home for paints and ammunition. I am now 86 years of age and was in all the Indian depredations until the treaty of 1867.
>
> The beginning of the Black Hawk War was caused by John Lowery whipping an Indian (about 1863 or 1864) at the grist mill some distance from Manti.
>
> The Indian went from the mill down to Six Mile Creek and killed a young man from Manti which started the war.
>
> One of my most exciting experiences was on November 24, 1865 my husband, James W. Munson and I went to Salt Lake City from Circleville to receive our endowments and get our winter supplies. There were several others in our company, among them my little brother, my sister and her husband, Mads Nielsen.
>
> On our return home we got within about 8 miles of Circleville when we espied the Indians driving off our stock. I asked my husband to get me a piece of ice, the excitement had made me so thirsty. But ice did not quench my thirst. At this time we heard a gun go off and my husband said 'They have killed old man Floyd.' He was a man who had been riding with us but he got out of our wagon and thought he

would go ahead of us to town. When we got to the top of the hill we saw the wagon of my brother in law, Mads Nielsen and one horse was killed. The wagon was stripped of all its contents—it contained bedding and clothing and flour. The feather beds were ripped open and the feathers scattered to the four winds. The Indians had emptied out the flour sacks what they could not take with them and when I saw the heaps of flour I exclaimed, 'They have killed my little brother and my sister's husband and my sister and covered them with flour.'

My husband replied, 'They have not killed Mads, I just saw the top of his head in the bushes—he is bare headed.'

My sister had got into a slough of water so that if the Indians killed her husband she would drown herself. Our little brother was afraid of the water so she sat him on the bank with his little feet hanging down so she could pull him in with her if the Indians came upon them. Our little brother was three years old. My sister remained in the water from 2 o'clock until dusk—the slough water was rather warm.

Mads was in the bushes close by and he told me he was afraid they had captured me because he had seen me on the hill and there were two men with me one on each side of me. He thought they were Indians but they were only two men who had hid themselves from the Indians and we found them when we got to the top of the hill.

When we reached the banks of the river there were twelve Indians on horse back waiting to kill us. My husband said, 'You had better hide in the bushes' to which I replied, 'When I die I want to die on open ground.' Then he said, 'Well, then you load the pistols as fast as I shoot them,' to which I agreed. He then packed me across the river on his back. For some unknown reason the Indians made their way to the herd that was being driven by other Indians and didn't harm us. They claimed after the treaty that they hadn't seen us. We made our way homeward in safety and were gladly welcomed by everyone.

These same twelve Indians had killed four, two men and two boys between circleville and the place where we saw them. One was Mr. Floyd, the one who had been in our company. They shot him and after he was wounded they stripped him of his clothing and chased him up a ravine.

Another was Chris Christensen. They shot him in the back and he fell forward on his face in some sand in the river bed. When he was picked up the next day his face was all mashed and his nose was mashed right straight to his face.

Orson Barney, a young boy was shot in the back of the head part of his head being blown off. helped lay him out and we stuffed cotton in his hair to make him look better before his mother saw him.

The other boy who was killed was Nels Halesen. The next day these four bodies were gathered up by the people from Circleville.

These are a few incidents that I was a witness to among lots of others that I could relate before the Black Hawk War.

Eliza Marie Allred Munson (1934)

Her sister, Ellen Aurelia Allred Nielsen recorded a second version of the November 26, 1865 attack led by White Horse Chief:

in the fall of 1865 with a company of friends we made a trip to Salt Lake City. we took with us a load of grain on our jerney to the City. when we reach manti on our return home my mother who was with us was taken very ill and had to be left ther. her little two year old boy we took with us in our wagon. at monroe in Sevier county my sister and husband who were traveling with us left us and started home each having a team of our own. with us was a old gentleman named floyd. he had purchased a pair of steers and was driving them to his home in Castle valley. on the night of nove 25, we camped with a relative at marysvale. that night my husband was uneasy and restless and slept but little although he knew no reason for the same. in the morning my uncle with whom we had spent the night tried to persuade us to remain with them that day but we decided to go home and so started on our journey. my uncle told us afterwards that he felt so uneasy after we had left that he came very nearly following us to git us return. when we were within ten or eleven miles of our home we drove around and passed the other team which was driven by my brother in law. we were so near home we thought there was no danger. we were about three miles from town when we saw as we drove around the front of a hill a heard of cattle being driven towards the north of the canyon. I was very much frightened as soon as I saw them for fear it might be Indians driving the stock. I begged my husband to turn back but he said the Indians had seen us and that by driving fast that we might reach a company of men who were in persuit of the Indians. in a few minutes the Indians left the stock and with a yell started towards us. our horses were very tired but we urged them on thinking that we might reach a swamp about three fourths of a mile away.

but we did not succeed. the Indians came up and we was going to shoot up his band but we frightened him off a way by pointing an old revolver at him. I suppose I am safe now in telling that the revolver was an old broken one but we did not tell the Indians.

Mr. redskin now turned and shot our best horse which of course stopped the team. at the request of my husband I with my Brother in my arms jumped from the wagon, the

Indian was reloading his gun. There were willows along the road but were low and did not afford much protection. the Indian again mounted his horse and rode around trying to get a chance to shoot my husband. at this I jumped in to a slough that was near. the water was up to my neck but I prefered drowning to being captured by the Indians. my husband again pointed the revolver at the Indian and again he turned back. my husband then took my brother who I was holding and up out of the water and I jumped out of the slough. we walked down to try to cross the swamp at another point but were headed off by 10 indians. so we got in the water again. the little boy began to cry because the water was so cold and we left the slough again. I sat down behind a bunch of willows taking the child in my lap and my husband stood over us to give what protection he could .the Indians did not follow us into the willows but turned thur attention to wagon. they cut the harness from the dead horse leaving the collar. they took the wagon cover off and emptied all the flour on the ground, cut the feather bed tick and scattered the feathers all round, threw the dishes out of the wagon breaking all but one plate which I still have at home. they took all of our clothing. while they were destroying the things in the wagon the old gentleman floyd who was traveling with us arrived at the top of the hill and saw the indians. he might have escaped alright if he had gone back himself at once but he ran around his steers to drive them back and the Indians saw him and followed him in to the hills a mile and killed him. Just before my sister and her husband reached the ridge they were met by two men who had been sent out to guard the cattle. these men said while they were sitting in a bunch of willars eating their dinner the Indians came out of the canyon and seated themselves and held a council close to them. one of the men had a dog with him and he sat and held

> the dogs mouth to prevent him from making a noise and so they escaped being discovered. these men informed my brother in law that the Indians had made a raid on the settlement. as they traveled on through the hills my sister and husband found the body of old mr floyd whom the Indians had killed. when they reached the top of the hill they could see our wagon and the wounded horse lying by it. they thought we had been killed we were hidden in the willows and could hear my sister crying. my husband wandered out where he could see them and as he saw four persons he thought they were Indians and we dared not come out to them. it was geting dark and we had been ther since 2 o'clock in afternoon. We got out of the willows and started for the settlement. by another rout we reached our home about an hour after the others had arrived. it was late in the evening we were both bare headed and my clothes were frozen stiff. my brother had gone to sleep. we entered the house it was full of people who had gathered because of the report that we had been killed. it is needless to say that our meeting was a happy one. we were left almost destitute as the indians had destroyed what few things we had. for a bed we borrowed a wagon and filled it with straw and all we had for a bed was one quilt which we were fortunate to borrow. this served us during the winter of 1865 and 1866. in the spring of 66 the people were called to leave their homes and their grains which was up and growing nicely and return to Sanpete. this we did.

Earlier in the day, Eliza Marie Allred and Ellen Aurelia Allred's brother and sister, Edward Francis Allred and Elizabeth Diantha Allred and two other young boys, Orson Barney and Ole Heilersen were out in the fields herding cattle in the warm November sun when about noon the raiders attacked and killed Barney and Heilersen. They drove the stolen cattle up East Fork Canyon along the East Fork of the Sevier towards Grass Valley. Edward Allred ran into the town of Circleville to alert the residents of the attack on the two thirteen-year-old boys.

In an article in *The Deseret News* August 25, 1934, Eliza Marie Allred Munson's account of the incident is again recalled along with that of her sister, Elizabeth Diantha, her brother Edward Francis Allred and her cousin, John L. Allred:

> "He was greater than Black Hawk!" swear some of the hoary-headed veterans of the war, referring to the White Horse Chief. This Ute was the most daring of all the war chiefs, according to John L. Allred, a nephew of two prominent Indian interpreters. He was a fine-looking Indian. Besides being brave and handsome, he seemed to have a superstitious hold on his warriors. They claim-ed he had died, then miraculous-ly come to life, and they called him Shi-Nav-Egin, which means "Son of Diety" or "Son of the Sun", informs C.L. Christensen, Indian interpreter.
>
> He bore a grudge against the settlers because he claimes white boys from Manti crippled his son for life.
>
> He led the raid on Circleville on November 26, 1865, declares Mrs. Elizabeth Diantha Allred, now 82, who at 14 witnessed the raid. That day she and her brother Edward had been left to ride a horse and tramp out wheat on a farm some distance from town. They heard a shot. Edward stood erect on the horse to look about. He saw a band of Indians pursuing a small boy. The raiders overtook their prey and shot him down.
>
> Edward scurried into town to spread the alarm. Only six men were left in the hamlet at the time, tells Mr. Allred. Messengers swiftly summoned the people to the meeting house for safety. Herding livestock of the settlement together, the raiders encountered another lad searching for a

> cow. They killed him also. Then whooping and brandishing their weapons, they swept their plunder up toward the mouth of the canyon.
>
> Several miles from town they surprised a little caravan returning from Salt Lake City. Mrs. Eliza M. Munson, who was riding with her husband in the last wagon relates her experience.

Eliza Marie Munson ends the article with her account:

> Through some quirk of destiny, the Indians ignored or failed to see the frightened pair. The Utes dug heels into their ponies' sides and galloped off to join those driving the herd. The Munsons reached Circleville in safety. An hour later the Nielsens also arrived. They told a thrilling tale of their escape.

The article goes on to state:

> Small wonder that the settlers of Circleville remembered this day when trouble threatened again. Later they retaliated in a sanguinary way.
>
> This was the last serious depredation of the first year of the war. Black Hawk retired to the mountains in the southeast for the winter. But he has taken a heavy toll in human lives and livestock.
>
> The settlers were too scattered to resist the attack and gathered in the meetinghouse for protection and to plan their pursuit. A small force of settlers on foot and on horseback pursued the band but with no modern arms, Tamaritz was able to keep the settlers at bay with his Henry rifle, an early repeating rifle. Of those attacked by Tamaritz's warriors on the late November autumn day, only James Tillman Sanford Allred's family members survived. Eliza Marie Allred wrote,

> "When we got home at dusk we were gladly welcomed home even by the old squaws who kissed us although they had been our traitors."

James T.S. Allred knew Arapeen, who was brother of Sanpitch and Wakara. Arapeen, Sanpitch, Wakara and Sowiette were the most powerful Ute chieftains. Arapeen and Wakara were both dead before the beginning of the Black Hawk War, which began in 1865 and ended in 1872. Wakara, (Walker), which means yellow, died after being sick for ten days, most likely from pneumonia, January 29, 1855, at Meadow Creek. Wakara was buried with two imprisoned Paiute women and two imprisoned Paiute children, articles sent by Brigham Young and twenty of Wakara's best horses. After Wakara died, his brother Arapeen was made chief of the Ute Indian Tribe. The winter of 1855 found Brigham Young in poor health. In April of 1855, James T.S. Allred was called by "The Lion of the Lord" to serve a mission to Las Vegas.

*

The incident referenced as igniting the Black Hawk War, the most serious and long term conflict, began when John Lowry, an interpreter living in Manti and allegedly drunk, pulled Arapeen's son, Jake Arapeen, from his horse April 9, 1865. Chief Black Hawk, Sow-ok-soo-bet, An-kar-tewets, Toquana and Jake Arapeen had come to town to settle a dispute over some cattle that had been taken and butchered by the Indians. The harsh winter of 1864–1865 brought starvation as well as diseases contracted from the Mormon settlers decimating the Native Americans. Lowry called a meeting with Chief Black Hawk, Jake Arapeen and other Ute Indians. An argument ensued. Lowry grabbed Arapeen by the hair pulling him from his horse. Jake Arapeen strung his bow in defiance. Jake Arapeen and Lowry began fighting but were separated. Lowry went to get a gun. In response, Jake Arapeen and Chief Black Hawk yelled defiantly as the Ute party rode out of Manti.

Jake Arapeen was murdered years later near Ephraim, Utah. Chief Black Hawk, Antonga, died September 26, 1870, east of Spring Lake in Utah County.

Koosharem 3 writes about "Poisoning of Indians at Manti:"

> One time a man who lived near Price and Emery, Utah, came down into the valley near Manti. He could see the Indian camp there with the tipis all around. He noticed that there was no smoke coming out of them. He also noticed that no one was around. The horses were out in the meadows grazing and were not fenced in. when he arrived at the camp no one was there, just blankets and belongings. There were not even any dogs to be found. He went up toward Nephi and told the Indians about it. They told him that the white men had given the Indians poisoned meat and flour and it had killed them all. The white men had come and got the bodies.

As told by Koosharem 3 who heard this story from Walker Ammon, son of Chief Walker.

In James T.S. Allred's Diary from October, 1858 we have the following entry:

> Tuesday 26th I started south on a mission to the Indians & I traveled threw Manti City and on to the Indian farm 19 miles Wednesday 27th I traveled south 30 miles Thursday 28th I traveled south 35 miles Friday 29th I traveled south 30 miles and arrived at the Arapenes camp in the sever valley I had quite a long talk with him he treated me very kindly & friendly Saturday 30th I started back home and traveled 35 miles Sunday 31st I traveled 60 miles Monday November 1st 1858 I arrived at home traveled 19 mz

James T.S. Allred had a close association with the Native Americans and certainly this association was at the direction of and blessing from Brigham Young. As a member of the Mormon Church and as a member of the Utah Militia, Allred would view Brigham Young, the colonizer, governor and prophet, as his leader. The Native Americans had a common bond with the early Mormon pioneers, as they related to being driven from their land. The policy of friendship often failed, as the distance between the cultures, the dynamics of the expansion of the western frontier and the failures of individual human nature could not always be overcome.

General Daniel H. Wells reported, "from 50 to 70 settlers an equally large number of Indians … and a vast number of horses and cattle lost, killed or stolen." It wasn't until March 4, 1917 that the Black Hawk War Pensions were approved.

As is clear from his daughter, Eliza Marie Allred Munson's account, the family knew Chief Arapeen and Chief Black Hawk. Brigham Young called James T.S. Allred to learn the language of and preach the Mormon Gospel to the Native Americans. James T.S. Allred married his third wife, Fanny Shantaquint, a member of Ute Indian Nation, December 13, 1862. The couple had a daughter, Barbara, born February 14, 1860. On August 1, 1862, Brigham Young wrote to a local bishop:

> my advice is for bro James T. S. Allred to marry the Indian girl in question. It is written that 'not many generations shall pass away before they become a white and delightsome people'.

9

IT IS APRIL 22, 1866. THE AIR IS COLD at night and cool in the day. The nearby Sevier River is full with the spring run-off and crossing is difficult. The fields are green. The trees are still bare, with only a hint of green in the full sunlight. The willows along the river are springtime deep red and cast purple shadows. It is spring. It is in the fifties in the daytime and low to mid thirties at night at this elevation of 6,000 feet. A third of the month, the day is punctuated with spring showers. The earth is moist. The bright half-moon is eight days past the full moon, approaching the last phase of the moon. It rises around noon and sets near midnight. The light is bright enough to cast shadows in the night of this valley. The Circle Valley.

Two days before, on April 20, 1866, James T.S. Allred's wife of twenty-one years, Eliza Bridget Mainwaring Allred, forty-four years old, died six hours after giving birth to their tenth child, Margaret Bridget Allred who will be brought up by her older sister, Eliza Marie Allred Munson. The Allred household had consisted of James T.S. Allred and his three wives: Eliza Bridget and seven children, her sister Margaret and two children, Fanny Shantaquint Allred and her child.

James T.S. Allred and his son, Edward Francis Allred, were in Salt Lake City buying supplies when they received word that Eliza was dying. Edward Francis Allred, ten years old, was given a six-shooter and a few rations for the two hundred mile trip on horseback through hostile country. His father, James T.S. Allred, came as quickly as he could while driving the supply wagon. They said their good-byes on Eliza Bridget Mainwaring Allred's deathbed and quickly buried her.

On April 21, 1866, an express was sent from Fort Sanford to Circleville stating that two formerly friendly Paiutes had shot and wounded a member of the militia stationed at Fort Sanford. The fort had been completed in the spring of 1866 to help protect the scattered communities in this region and was named for its commander, Silas Sanford Smith. After receiving news of the attack at Fort Sanford, the settlers of Circleville met and decided to gather up the Paiutes living nearby and bring them in to town.

The Mormon Bishop, William Jackson Allred, second cousin to James T.S. Allred, sent word to the Paiutes requesting a meeting. It fell to Major James T.S. Allred, as commander of Circleville's militia, and as a reliable interpreter, to go and persuade the band of Paiute to come in to Circleville. Accounts differ as to whether all the "able bodied" men of Circleville went or whether two smaller groups of Circleville men, one consisting of Major James T.S. Allred, his younger brother, Andrew Jackson Allred and a man name Oluf C. Larson went separately to the Indian encampment. Oluf Christian Larsen wrote the following account:

> At this time our friendly Indians had not been in the valley for several days and we could not help being suspicious of them. They could easily have informed the others in regard to our condition. After they returned they camped close to town by the river where we observed some strangers coming and going from their camp. We naturally concluded the Indians were planning something. This led us to call a council to consider what was best to do about them. We concluded it was best to take them prisoners, feed and care for them until we could get information from higher authority. In the evening we went quietly down and encircled their camp. We closed up quite well, so none should be able to escape if they tried to break away. A man by the name of James Allred who spoke the Indian language very well, and who had had

considerable experience among them and knew their customs quite well showed them the necessity of complying with our wishes telling them they would be treated kindly and would show their friendship by moving into town. No sooner had he explained this than one Indian jumped across the river where I had my position and in the twinkle of an eye the man opened fire and the bullets whistled around my ears. Just as the Indian fell he discharged his gun. The bullet grazed my breast and cut the barrel square off the gun of the man by my side. Had the bullet come three inches nearer it would have killed both of us. All the other Indians surrendered and we marched the men into the meeting house and we placed them under guard. Later we went and moved the squaws and children and belongings into a vacant cellar with guards watching them.

Express was sent across the mountains to Beaver, the nearest place we could get in communication with the leading authorities as we did not like to take the responsibility of deciding the course to be take with the Indians. While thus being guarded night and day and they knowing we could not understand them they held their council how to liberate each other. The plan they made failed and brought upon themselves an early destruction for if they had depended on us they might have been liberated in a few hours receiving gifts from us. A few men in the community exhibited great hatred to the Indians, but they were too few to have any influence as the people in general abhored the shedding of blood.

Every moment we expected our pony express to return but before they returned the Indians made a bold break for liberty. The Indians were seated with sticks across the small of their backs and elbows back of the sticks were tied to the sticks. While close together with blankets thrown across their

> shoulders they untied each other and were loose ready to make their escape as soon as it was dark. I had just been released and the new guard place—had not proceeded far when the shooting began. I ran back to the meeting house and the Indians were all shot and in a dying condition. I learned from the guard that they all arose at once pulled the sticks from their arms, sprang for the guards and tried to knock them down. To protect themselves they were forced to shoot. The next consideration was how to dispose of the squaws and papooses.
>
> Considering the exposed position we occupied and what had already been done it was considered necessary to dispatch everyone that could tell that tale. Three small children were saved and adopted by good families.

Some of the male Indian prisoners were shot during the attempted escape. Those who were not shot were taken one by one, hit with a club and knocked out, their necks broken and their throats slit. One child was beaten over a wagon wheel.

Koosharem 3, of the Southern Paiutes heard this story of the Circleville Massacre from Walker Ammon, son of Chief Walker:

> There used to be a big old log house in Circleville, Utah, beside the road where it curves near where the potato cellars are. Years ago the white men at Circleville locked up in that house all the Indians who were living nearby and told them they were going to cut their throats. They began doing this by taking them outside one at a time and cutting their throats. There were two young men inside who decided they were going to escape. One said to the other, "We will have to dash through them and run just as they open the door." They did this and ran through the white men who were gathered around them. They ran towards the cemetery on the hill to the

north and as they were going over it, one of the pursuing white men on horseback shot one of the Indians in his side by the ribs but it was only a flesh wound. From there they ran up into the mountains and then the wounded Indian put some Indian medicine on his wound and wrapped it in part of his shirt. The white men didn't follow them far so from there they went on over to Parowan or Beaver.

On May 5th, 1866 William Jackson Allred wrote to George A Smith describing the events at Circleville:

> I take this opportunity to write you a few lines to let you know how we are getting along in Circleville. After I left you in SanPete I returned home. I called the brethren together and laid before them the subject of moving close together which was agreed to and we commenced to move our houses about the 23rd of April. We received an express from Major S.S. Smith stating that two of our friendly Indians had shot one of his men by the name of West and that one of the Indians had been killed. We immediately sent to the Camp and requested them to come in to town which some of them did. I informed them of what we had learned by the express. I further told them that it was our wish to live in friendship with them and if this was the desire to live in peace with us I wished them to loan us their guns and go to work for us and we would pay them in such things as they stood in nead of as they had told me they had not a charge of ammunition we would take their guns and defend ourselves and stock but they refused to do either. After reasoning some time with them I took their arms which they parted with reluctantly. Major J.T.S. Allred placed a guard over them and then returned to the camp to look for two more Indians who were reported to be there. When they reached camp the two

Indians cocked their guns and started off. They were told in their own language that they would not be hurt but they started to run and one of them was shot down. He fired in return and slightly wounded one of our men. The whole band was taken then and disarmed And put under guard and word sent to Colonel Dame. The Indians confessed to be carrying ammunition to hostile Indians. They say that Black Hawk is at the Red Lake or Fish Lake from 40 to 60 miles from Circleville with a large amount of stock and that the Pi Utes, Pahvants and the Navajoes have agreed to unite against us as a people that our little valley will be full of them of the 24th. At night fall our prisoners rushed on the guard with clubs striking them with the same. The guard killed 16 of them which was all of the band except four children which we have yet. We think of sending them north to some of the settlements. We are all in a fort around the meeting house and we feel to maintain our ground. About 40 head of horses and cattle have been taken by the Pi Utes from Marysvale and the families are in this place. Some of the people think we will have to leave here. A word from President Young or yourself of encouragement to the people would greatly assist me in holding our ground. We have had no word from the Col. I called on Major S.S. Smith to assist us but he could not let them go.

Yours truly,
William J. Allred

William Jackson Allred, the first bishop of Circleville, eventually resettled in Beaver, Utah. On November 10, 1868, he got up to find his horses missing and tracked them through several canyons when he discovered smoke. He came upon three Indians. He fired at two but one got away. William Jackson Allred dragged the bodies of the two dead men together and covered them with sagebrush set their bodies on fire. He recovered his horses and returned home that night.

*

A story that circulated among Circleville settlers recalled that one Paiute boy escaped being killed by climbing up the chimney of the meetinghouse. He returned to Circleville boasting of his feat to a Circleville resident who then hired him to dig a pit down by his orchard. When the pit was finished, the Circleville resident killed the Paiute and buried him in the grave dug by his own hands.

Peter Gottfredson, who was "personally acquainted with conditions in Sanpete and Sevier Valleys during the years 1863 to 1872", and who was personally acquainted with James T.S. Allred, wrote this account of the "Indians Killed At Circleville" in 1919:

> Although the Indian depredations were raging in all directions and many murders had been committed by Black Hawk and his band the year before, the Piute Indians still remained in Circle Valley professing friendship, although they were mistrusted by many of the settlers. Some of their actions were so suggestive that the whites felt themselves in danger every moment, not knowing when a break would be made by these savages on the settlement. On Saturday, April 21, 1866, an express reached Circleville with the news that two of the pretended friendly Piutes had shot and killed a white man who belonged to a party of militia stationed some distance up the Sevier River at Fort Sanford. This fort, which had been built that spring by the militia under the direction of Silas Sanford Smith, was about half way between Circleville and Panguitch. Word was immediately sent to the people of Circleville to protect themselves against the Indians who were camped in their valley. On receiving this admonition, the men

of Circleville settlement were called together for consultation, and after considerable deliberation it was concluded as the best policy to place the Indians encamped near their settlement under arrest. Consequently, all the able-bodied men of Circleville were mustered into service, some on horseback and some on foot. Thus organized they proceeded to the Indian camp, which they surrounded after dark. They had no trouble or occasion, however, to use force as James T.S. and Jackson Allred went into the Indian camp and persuaded the savages to come to the meetinghouse in Circleville to hear a letter read, which had just been received. All the Indians complied willingly with this request, with the exception of one young Indian warrior who not only refused to go but commenced to shoot at the posse, who returned the fire and killed him; the rest of the Indians were guarded in the meeting house that night. The letter brought in by express was then read to the Indians who were told that they would be retained as prisoners, awaiting further particulars of the killing of the white man at Fort Sanford. The Indians showed resistance, but their bows, arrows and knives were taken from them, and thus secured the boys took turns guarding them through the night.

Toward evening of the next day (April 22nd), while the Indians were still being guarded in the meetinghouse, some of them succeeded in getting loose and immediately commenced an attack upon the guards, knocking two of the men down. There was every reason to fear a general break on the part of the Indians, and it was decided that the settlement of Circleville would be in great danger if the Indians were allowed to escape. In the general melee and excitement which followed the Indians were killed, with the exception of a number of children, who were taken care of by the settlers.

> After this sad affair there were no more attacks on Circleville on the part of the savages, but companies of militia arrived in the valley from other parts of the Territory to assist the settlers in defending themselves, and a strong guard was kept around the town after that. As there was constant danger from attacks by the Indians, the settlers had built their houses in fort style around the meeting house, a short distance east of where Bishop Peterson lives at this writing. The settlers from Marysvale moved into Circleville that summer, but as the danger from attack by Indians became greater than ever, instructions were finally given by the authorities of the Church and the men in charge of the militia of the Territory, that Circleville, as well as the other places on the Upper Sevier, would be vacated and the people moved to older and stronger settlements for safety. About forty families were at that time living at Circleville. The evacuation took place June 20, 1866, most of them going north to Sevier and Sanpete Counties, while a few crossed the mountains on the west to Beaver and other places, leaving their fields of promising grain behind unharvested, about 700 acres of land was under cultivation at the time. About fifteen families constituted the population at Marysvale, but it is not known how much land they had under cultivation when they left their settlement, first to seek refuge in Circleville and afterwards to vacate that place again for other parts. The fields thus left with growing wheat and vegetables were afterwards harvested by people from Beaver who came over the mountains for that purpose.

In John Franklin Tolton's memoir *From the Halls of Memory* he writes in 1931, at age of seventy years, of his early childhood in Circleville:

Some ten days prior to the abandonment of Circleville, there occurred some thrilling episodes which riveted themselves upon my mind, though I was but a child of four and one half years old.

One day as I climbed upon our low log house, using for a ladder the projecting ends of the logs upon the corner of the house, I saw father, about three hundred yards away, coming towards home at full speed, holding to the tails of the oxen, which he had been using to do some plowing.

In the midst of the Indian trouble every man provided himself with a gun, rifle, or shot gun, and this he carried with him at all times, whenever he was absent from home, or working in the fields. while my father was plowing near home, but on the opposite side of the river, which at this point was about 100 feet wide, Blackhawk, with some twenty followers, rushed down from the foothills on horseback, about a half mile distant. The oxen were attracted by the scent of the Indians, which made them restless and unmanageable. Father at once unhitched them, and taking a tail of an ox in each hand, made haste for home.

Upon reaching the river, the oxen plunged in and swam to the opposite shore, father holding his gun above his head to keep the powder dry during the swim. None too soon he reached the opposite bank and took refuge in a thicket of bullberry bushes, just as the Indians reached the river bank opposite. Pointing his gun in their direction, in a threatening manner he caused them to retreat to a safe distance beyond range of the gun. They departed up the river about a quarter of a mile, still in range of my vision, and met a man and boy who were homeward bound with a load of wood. The Indians surround the wagon, filling the bodies of the man and boy with arrows causing their immediate deaths, and then made off, taking the yoke of oxen which were hitched to the wagon. This was the first sight I had witnessed of the taking of human life.

The final act in the great drama occurred a week later. About 30 supposedly friendly Indians were bound and imprisoned in the "blockhouse" which was located in the center of the rectangle forming the Fort, with an armed guard of three men on duty, among whom was my father.

While I was playing near the entrance to the blockhouse, my attention was attracted by the sound of Indian war whoops from the inside, and the sounds of scuffling men, and benches breaking. Seeing the door slightly ajar, I rushed over to it and pushed it open and went in. I soon discovered that I was in the midst of great commotion. The Indians and guards were engaged in a life-and-death struggle. One of the Indians and guards, Hy Fowler, discovering my presence and great danger, caught me by the seat of my pants and threw me out the door. The tumult, as I learned later, was caused by the fact that several of the Indians had, with the use of a knife, cut the thongs which bound their arms, before they were discovered by the guard. Though their feet were still bound, they outnumbered the guards and were subdued only when they had been knocked unconscious by the clubbing with guns by guards. Had a few more Indians secured their freedom of hands, before being discovered, it would have resulted in the deaths of the guards and possibly the entire colony.

These Indians were charged with treason and were tried, convicted, and executed by due process of law, and their bodies buried in an old cellar near the entrance to the Fort. This was the final act leading to the Blackhawk uprising.

Though I was but four and a half years of age at the time, I recall even late in life, our home and environments at Circleville, and many incidents of my life there.

10

JAMES T.S. ALLRED WAS RESPONSIBLE for bringing the Paiutes into Circleville with the promise of safety. He then sent an express to Colonel Dame requesting orders as to what to do with what were now their Indian prisoners. From Oluf Christian Larsen's account, we gather the prisoners were held the night and the next day and in the next evening they were killed. It is documented that on Sunday night April 22, 1866, James T.S. Allred was part of a group of militiamen tracking Indians who had stolen livestock by following the trails of their lariats dragged on the ground. They were ambushed and attacked by the Native Americans outside the Marysvale fort in early dawn on April 23, 1866. James T.S. Allred was attending to the mortally wounded Christian Christensen. Peter Gottfredson, who knew James T.S. Allred, writes in his *Indian Depredations of Utah*:

> The company rode up to the Fort, leaving Wilkenson with the dead and wounded men. Shortly Major Allred and Peter Christensen (Christensen's brother-in-law) returned and Wilkinson and Allred then formed a chair by crossing their hands (one man holding the wrist of the other) and carried the wounded man up to the fort while Peter led the horses. Lewis was left where he fell till morning, which was not long. The Indians took the cattle and drove them up the Valley southward. The company followed and when up five or six miles they saw the Indians driving stock up what they called Rock Canyon across the valley eastward. It was probably the

> east fork of the Sevier river. There, on a ridge, they met about forty men from Circleville. Next a council was held to decide whether the men should follow the Indians into the mountains and try to recover the stock, or turn back. They decided on the latter course, the Circleville people going home and the others returning to the Vale (Marysvale).

James T.S. Allred, with the militia, tracked the stolen stock along an Indian trail on the ridge of the mountains as far as the East Canyon of the Sevier River, which is northeast of Circleville. Forty men from Circleville met him. After some discussion, most probably about the massacre that had taken place, they decided to return to Circleville.

The original message from Fort Sanford was sent on April 21st, 1866. After receiving the message, the settlers of Circleville met. They would waste no time acting on the information contained in the message and gathered the Paiutes. Their arrival was announced by the sound of their horses as they covered the rocky terrain. James T.S. Allred, Andrew Jackson Allred, Oluf C. Larsen and a posse of Circleville men brought the prisoners in to Circleville. The first group consisted mainly of Paiute men followed by a second group consisting of the remaining men and the women and children. The men were placed under guard in the meetinghouse and the women and children placed under guard in a cellar for the night. From Oluf Christian Larsen we learn the prisoners were "guarded night and day" and "were loose and ready to make their escape as soon as it was dark".

James T.S. Allred sent his message to Colonel William H. Dame in Beaver. Travel over the Tushar Mountains to Beaver and back to Circleville with a good express rider on a fast horse would take two days. Given the current hostilities, an express rider would not be sent alone at night so the message was most likely sent at daybreak. On April 22, 1866, James T.S. Allred left for Marysvale, twenty miles to the north, which would take five to six hours on horseback. Here he met with twenty other militiamen from Richfield, Alma and Glenwood who were engaged in tracking Native Americans who had attacked Marysvale.

Peter Gottfredsen in his book, *Indian Depredations of Utah*, confirms James T.S. Allred was aiding the mortally wounded Christian Christensen. The date of this encounter is reliable as we have the death of Albert Lewis, who was killed in the ambush near the Marysvale fort on April 23, 1866. James T.S. Allred was not expecting a message from Colonel William H. Dame for a few days giving him time to respond to the call for militiamen to aide in the defense of Marysvale. James T.S. Allred had to leave in the early afternoon in order to reach Marysvale by evening.

He left the Paiute prisoners in a vulnerable situation when he left Circleville. The only other interpreter was his younger brother, Andrew Jackson Allred. When James T.S. Allred was met on the mountain coming home from Marysvale, the Paiute had been murdered. Forty men would not leave town when guarding a group of prisoners with an attack imminent. The discussion that took place on James T.S. Allred's return to Circleville was the Circleville posse telling Allred after the fact. The posse may have been tracking Paiute who had escaped capture so there would be no witnesses to the massacre.

The letter of request sent to Colonel Dame arrived when he was in company with General Erastus Snow, who wrote in a letter May 28, 1866 to General Daniel H. Wells:

> I left instructions with Col. Dame to see that those prisoners were treated kindly and such only retained in custody as were found hostile or affording aid to the enemy.

He also stated in this letter that he regretted not instituting an investigation and knew nothing officially about the incident but had learned about the "slaughter of 15 or 18 Piede prisoners".

In the Utah State Archives, Militia Records, there exists a cover for an express dated June 4, 1866, presumably to General Daniel H. Wells, from Warren S. Snow, who served as Brigham Young's scapegoat when enforcing severe policy toward the Native Americans and who symbolized hostility in their eyes. The contents are described as "enclosures from Circleville". There is no other documentation of these enclosures.

Regardless of what James T.S. Allred, Governor Charles Durkee, Superintendent of Indian Affairs in Utah F.H. Head, General Daniel H. Wells, Erastus Snow, Warren Snow or Brigham Young knew, no action was taken to investigate or to make amends for the Circleville Massacre. In a letter dated May 13, 1866, Thomas Callister of Fillmore wrote that Kanosh, chief of the Pahvants, "thinks that the Indians have sufficient cause to lose confidence in our promises of protection to friendly Indians." The event strained relations between white settlers and Native Americans for generations.

As reported in Reddick Newton Allred's letter to Major Seeley:

> Spring City, April 27th, Midnight
>
> Major Seeley:
>
> We have just received an express from the central station that Indians attacked Alma Sunday night. No particulars of the attack. The men from Richfield and Glenwood pursued the Indians and at the corner of Marysvalefield, were fired upon by the Indians, killing Alfred Lewis and wounding three other men. They then pursued the Indians up the canyon leading to Grass Valley. The Indians attacked the settlers of Circleville, taking twenty-five head of cattle, two mules and two horses. The men were at once in pursuit of them and followed them up into the canyon, but could do nothing as the Indians had secured positions and it would not be safe to attack them. We learned also, that the Indians had fired upon two of our men at Bear Creek above Circleville, wounding one slightly. The other man shot and killed one Indian and wounded another. Allred, of Circleville,

> took two bucks, six squaws, and six papooses tying them hand and foot, and on the 22nd they broke the cords that bound them and sprung upon the guards. The guards fired upon them killing all but four papooses.
>
> I think we will have to take the field and order men to be on hand. You will prepare at once, without delay, in case of a forward move. Captain Ivie will take charge of the men. I have suggested to the General the impropriety of drawing our men from here while we are menaced by the Indians from Spanish Fork Canyon. We shall make no draft upon Fairview. We shall want them to be prepared in case of an attack. Please copy and forward to Major Larsen of Fairview.
>
> Yours truly,
> Col. R.N. Allred

The report was filed close to the date of the incident and came via central express most likely from James T.S. Allred as head of the local Circleville militia. The number killed being sixteen as reported in William J. Allred's letter is also confirmed when we add the Paiute Indians that were killed when the posse first engaged the camp. This is most likely a conservative estimate as Toltin's account states "about thirty" Paiute weretaken prisoner.

James T.S. Allred promised the Paiutes safety and then placed them in a vulnerable position when he left town. There were people in the community who "exhibited great hatred to the Indians". The head of the Utah Militia, General Daniel H. Wells, was a friend of James T.S. Allred's and performed the marriage ceremony between James T.S. Allred and Perlina Jane Coy Allred in 1875, as documented in his application to the Department of the Interior in 1903, requesting a pension for his services in the Mormon Battalion, The Walker War and The Black Hawk War. When General Daniel H. Wells heard the report of the killings in Circleville, his response was he "could not well see how the brethren there … could have done less." Wells visited

Circleville in the summer of 1866 and thought the location dangerous and the settlement premature.

Responses to the incident varied. Some viewed the action as heinous. Others felt it a just response. Brigham Young took no immediate action but a decade later he thought the valley was cursed as "a band of our Lamenite brethren and their families, were here cruelly slain." Others felt that settlers in the community "were in league with the hostile Indians and should receive the same treatment."

This must reference James T.S. Allred. He was married to a Ute woman. He had children with this woman. He had an adopted Paiute son, Nephi. He spoke the Ute and Paiute languages. And he had been selling paint and ammunition to the Indians.

James T.S. Allred writes in his diary referencing Nephi on January 17, 1859:

> Sunday we had good instructions by the apostles in the evening I attended the church meeting Monday I returned home & When I arrived I found that my Indian boy had stolen my bro Reubens horse and ran away & Reuben followed him in the evening I attend meeting & after wards council and in the council Ephraim was disorganized & CG. Edwards was chozen to act as our future Bishop & President Protem Tuesday 18th I attended meeting We had good instructions in the after noon bro Reuben arrived home with my boy he got him in Nephi City

On March 13, 1859 James T.S. Allred's diary records:

> Sunday 13th cold & clear this night my Indian boy ran away with the soldiers

James T.S. Allred's wife, Fanny Shantaquint Allred did not accompany her husband to Spring City, Utah, but remained behind in

Circleville. She died November 1, 1866, after giving birth to an infant daughter, Hannah Allred, who was born and died in October of 1866. Fanny Shantaquint Allred was twenty-three years old. She and her child rest in unmarked graves somewhere near Circleville, Utah. Fanny Shantaquint Allred must have been able to tell the Native Americans of the events in Circleville.

James T.S. and Fanny Shantaquint Allred's daughter, Barbara, did accompany James T.S. Allred's household to Spring City. She married a cousin and died November 27, Thanksgiving Day in 1902, of pulmonary tuberculosis, and is buried in an unmarked grave in Mount Olivet Cemetery in Salt Lake City, Utah. The cemetery was a gift from the United States Government as an alternative burial ground to the Salt Lake City Cemetery. There is no mention of Fanny Shantaquint Allred on James T.S. Allred's tombstone in the Spring City Cemetery.

11

A YOUNG BOY, WHO WAS SPARED, was taken by James T.S. Allred's younger brother, Andrew Jackson Allred. After leaving Circleville and returning to Spring City, Andrew Jackson Allred traded him for two and a half bushels of wheat to Peter Monson who named him David Monson. David Monson grew up in Spring City, Utah. In his history his children wrote:

> David later told his children told how he had witnessed the slaying of his little sister—how she had been picked up by her heels by the whites and slung over a wagon wheel until she was dead. David never got over the horror of the massacre.

David Monson was raised in one of the loveliest houses in Spring City, Utah, built by Peter Monson, a Swedish immigrant and his wife Bertha, a Norwegian immigrant. He was raised with their daughter Petrea, who had been tragically scarred from a burning accident. The children were about the same age. In his history it also states that he told his children the name of the man who brought him to Sanpete as he wanted them always to remember his name.

David Monson lived in Spring City, Utah until he was sixteen or seventeen years old. David Monson never attended school so he could not read or write but he spoke English, Norwegian, Swedish and Danish. The Monson family records his baptism into the Mormon Church on July 4, 1874, age thirteen years old, by James T.S. Allred.

Mormon Church records state the date of his baptism in 1869, at the age of eight years old making his birth year 1861. David Monson lived in Spring City, Utah until 1877, when he went to help settle Castle Valley, Utah. He was described as being "strong, healthy and industrious", and five feet ten inches tall with high, cheekbones and a long oval face. He returned to live in Spring City.

On July 1, 1887, David Monson married a Danish girl named Laure Line Jensen. David Monson was twenty-five years old and Laure Line Jensen was fifteen and a half years old. She was fair skinned, petite and beautiful, having blue eyes and long, blonde hair.

She was also my great grandfather Daniel Jensen's sister. They were married with Laure's parents, Niels Peter and Ellen Marie Rasmussen Jensen as witnesses. They each signed the certificate with an "X." Niels Peter Jensen made them a lovely wedding cake, as he had been a member of the baker's guild in Denmark before migrating to America. They put down their roots in Spring City and lived in a log cabin at 55 South 500 East, under the shade of cottonwood trees beside a trickling irrigation ditch. Together they had eight children. Their daughter Edith Monson wrote of her childhood:

> We lived in a one room log house in Spring City. What a happy childhood we had even though we were very poor. Mother always said that 'We lived from hand to mouth.'

She wrote of her father:

> He was a gentleman who was fun loving and liked to attend the occasional picnic and dance. He liked to call out the dances played to the music of Jimmy Riddle, (John Davis), playing violin and Lute Zabriskie on banjo.

David Monson's adopted sister, Petrea, married Lars Louis Larsen, also a member of Spring City's Danish community. Their families remained close as children in each family were of similar ages.

David Monson earned his living working as a butcher and teamster. He hauled logs from Spring City Canyon. He also sheared sheep. In April and May of every year he would ride the train with companions from Spring City to Rawlins, Wyoming, where they sheared wool. In the spring of 1912, David Monson left Spring City for Wyoming to shear sheep. He never returned. He left Laure, forty years old and his wife of twenty-five years, with five children to support. Harold Cleve Monson who was eight months old, Mae Areah Monson was five years old, Bertha Saria Monson was eleven years old, Arthur Leroy Monson was fourteen and David Leonel Monson was seventeen. Their oldest daughter, Edith Elnora Monson, had married and left home in 1911.

In the Jensen Family Record Book, David Monson is listed as, "David Monsen," born in 1863. David Monson died February 15, 1925, of heart disease in Saratoga, Wyoming. His frozen body was found beside his beaver traps.

David Monson had no Paiute relatives who could testify on his behalf so members of the Spring City community signed an affidavit in 1964 confirming the fact that David Monson was a member of the Paiute Tribe in order for he and his descendants to receive reparations from the federal government. David Monson's descendants of up to and including one quarter Paiute were declared members of the Koosharem Band of the Paiute Indian Tribe. In Bergetta Jensen's affidavit written on March 6, 1964, she stated:

> This was told to me by my Mother Petrear Monsen Larsen. It was her parents Mr. & Mrs. Mons Peter Monsen that raised David Monsen the Indian Boy: "My Father was so desirous of having a Boy that he bought this Indian Boy for Two and a half bushel of wheat. It

> was in the year 1868. A man by the name of Jack Allred who brought this Indian Boy up from Marysvale, Utah said his Father and Mother and his whole Family were killed but this Boy. Jack Allred said that he was going to kill him if my Father did not take him. These Indians seemed to be more peaceful a Tribe than most of the other tribes were. They figured he was about six years old when they got him. And that he was a Piute Indian."

My grandfather signed his name, Daniel L. Jensen, 72, and my grandmother signed her name, Lafern Jensen, 68 yrs. There were twenty signatures of predominantly Scandinavian surnames. In a census taken in 1955, there were approximately 102 Paiute Indians living in the state of Utah. Of that, there were 34 members of the Koosharem Band.

My father told me in high school someone he did not know would greet him as "cousin". He learned this person was a grandson of David Monson. My grandmother told me the Monsons were "shirt tail relations" and would explain that my great grandfather's sister married one of the Monsons. My grandmother would tell me that she knew that there had been some kind of trouble but that she never knew what had happened, and that her grandfather had gone down to Circleville to bring his wife's body to Spring City for reburial.

12

On June 1st, 1866 Captain A. G. Gownover wrote to Col. William Pace:

> I arrived here yesterday about 10 o clock A.M. We met Major Allred out some distance from town with an escort, I ascertain'd from him that Col Smith was not here, I gave Col Smiths letter to him, Major Allred read it, then forwarded it with express. Predt Wm Allred wrote how the state of affairs stood here to Col Smith, He received answers from S.S. Smith to the amount that Col Smith has gone to Richfield. We found things in a very unsettled condition, as near as I can learn, there is very near half of the people here wish to evacuate this place; there is but 20 or 24 coming here from Panguish, there is some here that say they will leave anyhow. The people here don't know what to do, to illustrate affairs, just imagine the evening and next morning after we met Col McClellans camp on Cherry Creek, and you can draw a faint idea of the condition here.
>
> I have come to the conclusion that the only way to settle it, is for positive and emphatic orders to be sent here from a proper source. The people generally wish to obey council but immagine a few I, so, d_s' in their midst stirring up stryfe. From what I can see and learn, it would not be safe to undertake to sustain this place with less than 50 well armed men, over and above the forces of Panguish and Circleville. Ther is about 68 efficient men here now, but if those who saz

> they are going to leave do so, and the 24 from Panguish come down it will leave the place in the same condition they are at present.
>
> Bp Allred is writing to Col Smith now, Genl Pace please see Genl Snow and let him know how things are here and get instructions and send by Telegraph because it is with us very much, "I don't know, I tink so."
>
> The boys all feel first rate at present, but when this 20 days in this place are up, can't say, as some of them are already getting (word obscure).
>
> You must write on receipt of this all the answrs, and if you have none make some.
>
> Respectfully yours
>
> Signed A.G. Gownover, Captain.

In 1875 Circleville was resettled. There were four families living in or near Circleville. One of those families was Eliza Marie Allred and James Munson, who were the only members of the original settlers to return to Circleville after the evacuation. There were still over 700 acres of crops left to harvest. In Daniel H. Wells' narrative written in 1884, he wrote:

> Generally, however, we have found the cause of the hostilities have arisen from some imprudent or unwise act on the part of white men. It sometimes, however, would require the patience of Job to keep clear of trouble.

Wells makes no mention of Circleville. He merely states, "Hostilities continued through 1865–6".

In an express, Special Order No. 5 from Head Quarters SanPete Mil Expedition it states:

Circleville June 22d 1866
I. The Citizens of Circleville having concluded to remove their families and stock to more secure places of Safety Major Joseph Cluff is herby detailed with two platoons of men to remain and guard such persons with their Stock as wish to go to San Pete County

II. Campt Abram G. Gownover and Company are relieved from duty at Circleville and Capt Dalton of Fort Sanford is hereby ordered to move his company to Circleville and remain on duty to furnish guards for the families and Stock going to Parowan & Beaver

signed D.H. Wells
Lieut. Col. Nauvoo Legion

The Mormon and non-Mormon settlers of Utah had a history of ignoring atrocities. In 1857 Utah leaders took no action when 120 emigrants traveling from Arkansas to California were attacked at Mountain Meadows. Some claim it was a show of Mormon force meant to put the federal government on notice as to the power of the Mormon rule in the Territory of Deseret. In 1857 President Buchanan sent 2,500 troops to Utah to quash the rebellious Mormon community and to create a strong federal presence in the Territory of Deseret. In 1863 federal troops from Camp Douglas, acting under Colonel Conner, killed over 500 Shoshone Bannock Indians living near the Bear River in what is now southern Idaho. Corruption in the Department of Indian Affairs deprived Native Americans of supplies necessary for their existence further decimating their population.

13

THE UNITED STATES CENSUS UTAH TERRITORY Fort Ephraim June 16th, 1860 lists James T.S. Allred as a 33-year-old farmer with assets of 350 acres in real estate and 600 dollars as his personal estate. In his household are wife Eliza Bridget 38, his daughters Eliza Marie 12, Ellen Aurelia 10, Elizabeth Diantha 8, James T.S. Junior 6, Edward Francis 4, his second wife, Margaret 34, a seamstress, and Fanny, his third wife, 17 years old. The Census fails to mention his adopted Ute Indian son, Nephi Allred. The name Nephi Allred is listed on the House of Representatives 1st Congress 1st Session Mis. Doc No. 19.

> Payroll of Captain George Tucker's Company and cavalry, Utah Territory militia, employed in the suppression of Indian hostilities in Sanpete and Sevier counties, Utah Territory, from April 1 to November 1, 1866. We the undersigned, acknowledge to have received from James W. Cummings, paymaster Utah Territory militia, the sums set opposite to our names, in full payment for our services for the time specified.

Number 39 on the list is Nephi Allred, "rank do" ("ditto" for the rank above being that of a private)

> received $13 pay per month, $3.50 monthly allowance for clothing, $16.50 Total monthly pay and allowance, $84 for 40 cts. per day for use and risk of horse and horse equipment, $199.50 Total pay and allowance. Signed by Nephi Allred.

This company was mustered into service at Mount Pleasant, Sanpete County, April 1, 1866, by Brigadier General Warren S. Snow, and by him assigned to duty in the north and eastern mountains. They were on several expeditions to Fish Lake, Castle Valley, Green River, and up the Sevier River to Circleville. They were constantly scouting through the mountains, and on active service every day until mustered out, November 1, 1866.

On the pay roll of Captain Isaac M. Behunnin's company James T. S. Allred's name appears: 'Number 1. James T. S. Allred, rank 1st lieutenant, Total monthly pay and allowance $108.50, Total pay and allowance $759.50. Signed James T. S. Allred.'

This company was mustered into service at Springtown, Sanpete County, April 1, 1866, by Brigadier General Warren S. Snow, and by him assigned to duty in the vicinity of said city for the protection of life and property. They were in active service every day until mustered out, November 1, 1866.

I certify that the above account is correct.
H.B. Clawson, Adjutant General Nauvoo Legion.

After the Mormons were driven out of Missouri, Joseph Smith organized The Nauvoo Legion for protection from the "gentiles". The Nauvoo Legion melded into what became the Utah Militia once Utah became a United States Territory. Signatures on military records sometimes reflected past allegiances. The legislature of provisional government of the State of Deseret created Sanpete County on January 31, 1850. Statehood was granted January 4, 1896.

James T.S. Allred was placed in charge of his own company as captain, May 1, 1867 to November 1, 1867 and "employed in the suppression of Indian hostilities in Sanpete County, Utah Territory from May 1, 1867 to November 1, 1867" earning $129.50 in total monthly pay and allowance, $72.40 cents per day for use and risk of horse and horse equipment and earning $849 total pay and allowance.

Nephi Allred is listed as Number 6 on his list having earned $171 total pay and allowance. James T.S. Allred's adopted Paiute son, Nephi, ran away March 13, 1859, "cold & clear this night my Indian boy ran away with the soldiers." Other than this reference in Allred's diary we have no further record of Nephi Allred living in James T.S. Allred's home. Andrew Jackson Allred also had an adopted Paiute son named Nephi so there is some question as to which "Nephi" is referenced in the records.

A "Recapitulation of expenses incurred by the Territory of Utah in the suppression of Indian hostilities in said Territory during the years 1865, 1866, and 1867" include:

1865
Service rendered as per pay rolls $24, 194.76
Commissary supplies as per vouchers 6,849.98
Quartermaster's supplies as per vouchers 4,453.50
Transportation as per vouchers 7,518
$39,986.24

1866
Service rendered as per pay rolls $431,285.54
Commissary supplies as per vouchers 130,545.86
Quartermaster's supplies as per vouchers 30,832.43
Transportation as per vouchers 39,795
$632,458.83

1867
Service rendered as per pay rolls $300,112.19
Commissary supplies as per vouchers 102,198.42
Quartermaster's supplies as per vouchers 23,637.30
Transportation as per vouchers 22,644.40
$448,592.31
$1,121,037.38 Total

Supplies included vouchers for beef, bacon, flour, beans, rice, coffee, sugar, vinegar, candles, soap, salt, potatoes and molasses, bushels of oats, barley and hay.

Once again the United States Government was helping the Mormons carve out their Deseret, as it had done with the Mormon Battalion. Although in a letter dated May 3, 1866, signed by George Q. Cannon and Theodore McKean, the federal government is being chastised for not helping the settlers:

> It is remarkable that the government should have troops lying here idle in the vicinity of this city and be unwilling to use them to protect the settlements. Nearly 40 lives have been sacrificed in the Sanpete and Sevier Vallies by the cruel hostility of a band of marauders of the Utah Indians. We paid upwards of $41,000 of internal revenue tax, besides on freighters paid large sums in neighboring territories where they discharged their freight and received their pay.

On May 2, 1866, Brigham Young, Heber C. Kimball and Daniel H. Wells issued the following policy for members to observe when dealing with Native Americans:

> Dear Brethren, The recent occurrences in your counties and the threatened repetition of those scenes prompt us to write to you this epistle.
>
> To save the lives and the property of the people in your counties from the marauding and blood-thirsty bands which surround you, there must be thorough and energetic measures of protection taken, immediately.
>
> Many of your settlements at the present time are too weak to successfully resist attack, or to prevent their stock from being driven off by any band of Indians, however contemptible, who may choose to make a descent upon

them. These small settlements should be abandoned and the people who have formed them should, with out loss of time, repair to places that can be easily defended and that possess the necessary advantages to sustain a heavy population. There should be from 150 to 500 good and efficient men in every settlement; but not less than 150 well armed men; and their horses should always be where they can put their hands upon them. Where there are several settlements which do not have this number of men, there should be places selected at which the requisite number can concentrate. At all the points where the settlements are maintained, good and substantial forts, with high walls and strong gates, should be erected and the people moved into them.

Corrals also should be built, so convenient to the forts and in such a strong manner, that they can be easily guarded and the stock be kept safe in them from every attack.

In sending your stock on to the range, they should be placed in the charge of armed herdsmen and there should be enough of them to insure their own safety and the safety of the herds placed in their care.

When it is necessary for wood, poles or timber to be hauled, one or two persons should not venture into the canyons but a company should be formed who, well armed themselves, should also be accompanied by an armed escort. Before they enter into any place where there is the least danger of an attack, cautious men who can creep as close to the ground as any Indian, should precede them and reconnoiter, and while the men are at work, procuring their loads there should be other vigilant men stationed in commanding positions to maintain guard, and to give warning if danger should approach.

These precautions should also be observed strictly in the cultivation of your fields and upon every occasion when you may have to perform any labors that may require you to leave your Forts.

By breaking up your small settlements and gathering yourselves together in larger bodies you can observe these instructions and not feel that they are burdensome.

When settlements are abandoned measures should be taken to bury the house logs and fence poles, etc. to prevent their destruction of Indians. Holes can be dug of sufficient depth in which to put the logs, poles etc. and as they are buried, covered them with dirt, so that if the torch should be applied, they would not burn.

The grain in such places should be watched and the stock kept off and when it needs water or is ready to be harvested, enough armed men should go and perform these labors as to be safe.

The careless manner in which men have traveled from place to place frequently in parties of one, two or perhaps three and at times too when it was well known that the Indians were hostile, should be stopped and nobody should be permitted to venture out from home and from the protection of the Forts unless accompanied by a sufficient number of men to make traveling safe.

Adopt measures from this time forward that not another drop of your blood, or the blood of any belonging to you shall be shed by the Indians; and keep your stock so securely that not another horse, mule, ox, cow, sheep, or even calf shall fall into their hands, and the war will soon be stopped.

We wish to impress this upon your minds: put yourselves and your animals in such a condition that the Indians will be deprived of all opportunity of taking life and stealing stock, and you may rest assured that, when they find you have vigorously entered upon this labor and that they can gain no further advantage over you, they will soon cease their hostilities.

This policy which we now recommend has been urged upon the people for their adoption from the first formation of our settlements in these valleys until the present and in every instance where it has been strictly followed, life and property have been secure. On the contrary, where it has been neglected and men through their anxiety to possess large tracts of land and numerous herds of stock have gone off by themselves and have formed small settlements, life has been sacrificed and property destroyed.

The friendly Indians who are in our midst should not be ill treated, nor be made to expiate the wrongs of those who are hostile but if, while they are making professions of friendship to us they are our secret enemies and giving aid and comfort to those who are openly hostile, they should be treated as foes. If their friendship is real, they can give up evidence of it by informing us respecting the movements etc of the others which may come to their knowledge.

In giving these instructions and counsel, and making those requirements of you we do not ask you to do anything that we have not ourselves done. From the time that we left Nauvoo we have watched unceasingly; we built forts and guarded with diligence, and done for years all that you have done, or that you are now required to do and we never thought it hard; but have felt thankful for the privilege of performing these labors for the Gospels sake. Zion cannot be built and the kingdom of God be carried forward by us if we dwell at ease and are not diligent in the performance of our duties.

This directive was issued two weeks after the tragedy at Circleville. Certainly Brigham Young, Heber C. Kimball and Daniel H. Wells knew about the incident and formulated this policy as a partial response to those in the Mormon community looking for direction.

Military leaders signed "Utah Militia" or "Nauvoo Legion" and sometimes both below their signatures. In 1852 there were 2141 members registered on the Adjutant General's list, including 34 musicians, 27 buglers, 4 surgeons, 2 topographical engineers. The Second Legislative Assembly appropriated $50,000 to finance the legion. The legion was divided into 13 military districts in 1857. By July 1 1857, there were 6,000 members of the Nauvoo Legion. The Utah Militia's resources were bolstered in 1861 when federal troops abandoned Camp Floyd, the largest military camp in the United States, near Lehi, Utah. After 3,000 men evacuated camp, $4,000,000 worth of Army surplus was sold to the Mormon settlers for a small portion of its value.

In 1862 telegraph lines were being built and mail routes established between Missouri and California. President Abraham Lincoln sent a request to Brigham Young to aid the U.S. Government in protecting these lines of communication. Brigham Young responded:

> the militia of Utah are ready and able, as they ever have been, to take care of all the Indians, and are able and willing to protect the mail line if called upon to do so.

The troops were organized from a regiment of the Nauvoo Legion and three days later Brigham Young replied:

> Upon receipt of your telegram of April 27th, I requested General Daniel H. Wells, of the Utah militia to proceed at once to raise a company of cavalry and equip and muster them into the service of the United States army for ninety days, as per your telegram. General Wells forthwith issued the necessary orders and on the 29th of April, the commissioned officers and non-commissioned officers and privates,

> including teamsters, were mustered in by Chief Justice John F. Kinney, and the company went into camp adjacent to the city the same day.

The response of Brigham Young to Lincoln's request is in stark contrast to Lincoln's speech made in Springfield, Illinois, June 26, 1857 concerning the Dred Scott Decision:

> I begin with Utah. If it prove to be true, as is probable, that the people of Utah are in open rebellion to the United States, then Judge Douglas is in favor of repealing their territorial organization, and attaching them to the adjoining States for judicial purposes. I say, too, if they are in rebellion, they ought to be somehow coerced to obedience; and I am not now prepared to admit or deny that the Judge's mode of coercing them is not as good as any. The Republicans can fall in with it without taking back anything they have ever said. To be sure, it would be a considerable backing down by Judge Douglas from his much-vaunted doctrine of self government for the territories; but this is only additional proof of what was very plain from the beginning, that that doctrine was a mere deceitful pretense for the benefit of slavery. Those who could not see that much in the Nebraska act itself, which forced Governors, and Secretaries, and Judges on the people of the territories, without their choice or consent, could not be made to see, though one should rise from the dead to testify.

Lincoln goes on:

> If the people of Utah shall peacefully form a State Constitution tolerating polygamy, will the Democracy admit them into the Union? There is nothing in the United States

> Constitution or law against polygamy; and why is it not a part of the Judge's 'sacred right of self-government' for that people to have it, or rather to keep it, if they choose? These questions, so far as I know, the Judge never answers. It might involve the Democracy to answer them either way, and then go unanswered.

On December 31, 1867, the resources of the Nauvoo Legion are listed in the Adjutant Generals report as consisting of 9,207 infantry, 2,525 cavalry, 179 artillery and 113 engineers. Equipment included 2,838 horses, 252 swords, 77 trumpets, 96 fifes, 107 drums and 431,375 rounds of ammunition.

The military power of Nauvoo Legion came to an end on March 3, 1887, as part of the "Edmunds-Tucker Act" outlawing polygamy and also annulling the laws governing the Utah Militia.

Missourian Mark Twain visited Great Salt Lake City in 1872 on his way west to Nevada. He describes his first encounter with the Mormon pioneers in *Roughing It*,

> Just beyond the breakfast-station we overtook a Mormon emigrant train of thirty-three wagons; and tramping wearily along and driving their herd of loose cows, were dozens of coarse-clad and sad-looking men, women, and children, who had walked as they were walking now, day after day for eight lingering weeks, and in that time had compassed the distance our stage had come in eight days and three hours—seven hundred and ninety-eight miles! They were dusty and uncombed, hatless, bonnetless and ragged, and they did look so tired!
>
> However, time presses. At four in the afternoon we arrived on the summit of Big Mountain, fifteen miles from Salt Lake City, when all the world was glorified with the setting sun, and the most stupendous panorama of mountain

> peaks yet encountered burst on our sight. We looked out upon this sublime spectacle from under the arch of a brilliant rainbow! Even the overland stage-driver stopped his horses and gazed!

By the end of the visit, Mark Twain's enthusiasm for this "land of enchantment, goblins and awful mystery" is subdued after he encounters the Mormon community where he feels he is scalped, as nothing cost less than a quarter. Twain also meets "the King", Brigham Young:

> He seemed a quiet, kindly, easy mannered, dignified, self-possessed old gentleman of fifty-five or sixty, and had a gentle craft in his eye that probably belonged there. He was very simply dressed and was just taking off a straw hat as we entered. He talked about Utah, and the Indians, and Nevada, and general American matters and questions, with our secretary and certain government officials who came with us. But he never paid any attention to me, notwithstanding I made several attempts to "draw him out" on federal politics and his high handed attitude toward Congress. I thought some of the things I said were rather fine. But he merely looked around at me, at distant intervals, somewhat as I have seen a benignant old cat look around to see which kitten was meddling with her tail. By and by I subsided into an indignant silence, and so sat until the end, hot and flushed, and execrating him in my heart for an ignorant savage. But he was calm. His conversation with those gentlemen flowed on as sweetly and peacefully and musically as any summer brook. Then the audience was ended and we were retiring from the presence, he put his hand on my head, beamed down on me in an admiring way, and said to my brother: "Ah—your child, I presume? Boy, or girl?"

After his brief visit, Mark Twain concludes Utah is an absolute monarchy run by Brigham Young and The Book of Mormon is "chloroform in print". Twain left Great Salt Lake City:

> hearty and well fed and happy—physically superb but not so very much wiser, as regards the "Mormon question" than we were when we arrived …

*

Spring City, Utah was resettled in mid-July 1859. The town site consisted of 640 acres surveyed into blocks of seven acres each. In 1860, 220 people inhabited the settlement. The town was better prepared for the Black Hawk War, which broke out in April 1865, as they had constructed a rock fort for protection. But in May 1866 the settlers followed Brigham Young's advice and retreated to the safety of Fort Ephraim and the support of the settlers living there. The Spring City residents returned to Spring City July 24, 1866.

On August 13, 1867 while herding cows in the fields near the stone quarry, a group of men including Sanford Allred and Reuben Allred were attacked by a band of Indian warriors. They stampeded the livestock and killed two men, Martin Andrew Johansen and James Meek.

> Fort Ephraim Aug 14
> Pres. B. Young
> The Indians attacked some of the brethren on their way to the hay-field from Springtown. James Meek killed & Andrew Johnson dangerously wounded. Wm Blain shot through the ear—our scouts have all returned, one party came up with the Indians and had two or three engagements but could not…… Freed eleven and escaped with about thirty mostly

colts. Only twenty Indians here seen two or three supposed killed.

R.T. Burton & Wm. B. Pace

One of the final skirmishes of the Black Hawk War occurred near Spring City on September 26, 1867 when Daniel Morgan Miller was killed while he and his son were hauling timber from Oak Creek Canyon above Spring City. Miller's son had been wounded and was taken to the home of Reddick Allred in order to be tended.

On February 23, 1865, Congress enacted a treaty negotiating with Northern Utes removing their title to the Territory of Utah in exchange for a reservation in the Uintah Valley.

By 1867 most of the Uintah Utes, decimated by smallpox and other diseases, had been removed to the Uintah Reservation created in 1861 by President Abraham Lincoln.

The great Ute chief, Antonga Black Hawk, died September 26, 1870, blind and unable to speak and without his shaman. Prior to his death he had traveled throughout Utah expressing his sorrow to the white settlers. The treaty ending the Black Hawk War was signed September 17, 1872.

Head Quarters
Utah Military District
Springville City Sept. 23 1867.
Brig. Genl Wm B. Pace,

Dear Brother, yourself, together with your Brigade, will be, and appear at Camp Wells, on the Bench about one mile N.E. of Provo City, Utah County, on Monday the 4th of Nov, nest at 10 o'clk A.M. for the purpose of drill, inspection of arms, and Camp duty, break camp the Wednesday following at 2 o'clk P.M. You will cause all persons liable to do military duty within your command, to be en-rolled and notified. Delinquents will be dealt with as the law directs.

II. The Silver Grays at each Post or Settlement will act as home guard during the absence of the main force.

III. To ensure good order and sobriety you will instruct the officers under your command to use every precaution to avert the occurrence of accidents from carelessnes, negligence or otherwise.

IV. No ardent spirits will be allowed in or about the encampment during said muster.

V. You will cause vacancies of offices in the line, "if any" within your command to be filled during the said muster & make due return to these Head Quarters without unnecessary delay.

A. Johnson By Order of Lieut. Genl
Commanding
Utah Military District Nauvoo Legion

In 1867 there were 850 settlers living in Spring City, Utah. The peak population was 1,230 in 1900, including James T.S. Allred and his immediate and extended family.

14

JAMES T.S. ALLRED WROTE THE FOLLOWING OBITUARY for his father, James Allred, who died on January 10, 1876, in Spring City, Utah.

> DEATH OF A PATRIARCH IN ISRAEL Editor Deseret News: Father James Allred, son of William and Elizabeth Allred, died at Spring City, Sanpete County, Utah, January 10, 1876.
>
> Father Allred was born in North Carolina, Randolph County. January 22, A. D. 1784. He was married to Elizabeth Warren, November 14, 1803, and moved to Kentucky, Warren County. Two years afterwards moved to the Ohio River near Yellow Banks. In 1811 they moved to Tennessee, Bedford County. In 1830 they moved to Missouri, Rools County, which was afterwards divided into two counties, they living in Monroe County, and on the 10th day of September, 1832, he and the most of his family were baptized into the Church of Jesus Christ of Latter Day Saints, at which place a large branch of the Church was built up by G. M. Hinkle and others, and called Salt River Branch. In June, 1834, he went up in the Zion's Camp with the Prophet and others to redeem Zion. In September, 1835, he moved to Clay County, Missouri, and in the Spring of 1837 to Caldwell County, where he was elected County Judge, and also President of the Southern Firm.

When the Church left Missouri the Spring of 1839 he moved to Pittsfield, Pike County, Illinois. In the Fall of the same year he moved to Commerce, afterwards called Nauvoo, where he was ordained a High Priest, and a member of the High Council, and was one of the Prophet's life guards in the Nauvoo Legion. He also held several other responsible positions, helped to build the Nauvoo Temple, and assisted in giving endowments therein. On the 9th of February 1846, he crossed the Mississippi River to go west with the heads of the Church and others. He arrived at the Missouri River July 15th of same year, and here he was President of the High Council and acting Bishop at Council Point. In the Spring of 1851 he started to the mountain, arriving in Salt Lake in October of the same year, and went to Manti City, Sanpete County. In March, 1852, he moved to Canal, now known as Spring City, and was called to preside over this branch of the Church. At the Spring Conference of 1853 he was ordained a Patriarch in the Church of Jesus Christ of Latter Day Saints. In July the same year, the Indians drove the most of the cattle and horses off the belonging to the settlement, and on the last day of the month the settlers moved to Manti. In October they moved back to Canal with a company of Danish brethren, about forty families, and ten families of his own relatives. On the 17th day of December of the same year, he was called to vacate, and again move to Manti. In February, 1854, in company with fifty families, he commenced to build a fort on Cottonwood, now called Ephraim, of stone, ten feet high, which he finished, and presided over for some time. In 1860 he moved back to Canal, or what is now called Spring City, where he resided until his death. He was a faithful member of the Church, and strict in relation to the Word of Wisdom for over forty years. He fully endorsed all the principles of the gospel, as far as he knew them, was a very early riser, always on hand to obey the counsel of the servants of God.

"Mormanism" was his whole theme. For many years he was a regular attendant of quorum and public meetings, and always ready to donate to the poor, a friend to the widows and orphans and exemplary in his family, taught them to be honest, industrious, trustworthy and confidential. He told the Bishop that he was ready to join the U.O.[13] himself, and all that he had was on hand for the building up of the kingdom of God.

He raised twelve children of his own, and eight orphan children. All lived to have children of their own. He leaves the wife of his youth, after living together near 73 years, and a posterity of 447 souls, viz., 12 children, 104 grandchildren, 302 great grandchildren, 29 great great grandchildren, who sprang from the two. Five of his sons were present at his death, who are the only ones living.

He laid his hands on the head of his oldest son, the day before his death, and blessed him, who now is near 73 years of age. All of his children lived to embrace the New and Everlasting Covenant, and those who are dead died strong in the faith. The most of his posterity live in Utah, and are members of the Church. A large number of them have been baptized into the U.0.

He was 90 years old, lacking 12 days. His wife is year 90 years old, but has been blind for six years, and is healthy and strong at present.

The funeral took place on the 11th, and was the largest that has ever been in this place; 39 wagons and sleighs loaded with people followed him to his last resting place.

---

[13] United Order.

> President O. Hyde preached his funeral sermon and made some pertinent remarks touching the life, labors, and faithfulness of the Patriarch, which were satisfactory to his numerous family and friends. He died as he had lived, faithful to the Gospel of the Son of God.
>
> J. T. S. Allred

In 1889 in Sanpete County there were 414, 331 head of sheep 11,260 head of cattle, 4, 638 dairy cattle, 5,863, horses, 4,238 swine and an untold number of chickens. The major crops were: wheat 353,257 bushels, oats 135,077 bushels, barley 16,091 bushels, rye 4,170 bushels, corn alfalfa hay 27,985 bushels, wild hay 11,646 bushels, butter 212,522 pounds, cheese 8,180 pounds, honey 61,220 pounds, fruit trees 422 acres. And about 220 people lived in Spring City, Utah.

*

On March 4, 1905 James T.S. Allred applied to The Department of the Interior, Bureau of Pensions requesting an increase in his pension for his service during the Mormon Battalion, The Walker War and The Black Hawk War. He describes himself as married to Perlina Jane Allred.

> I am the claimant above named. For five years past I have been totally disabled for the performance of manual labor and there has been no one legally bound for my support. During the time my wife has owned no property. So have owned a small house in which we have lived with about 1 acre of ground attached. I own 58 acres of rocky land worth in all not over $400. This land is rocky and unfit for agricultural purposes and is entitled to one half water right clm 187. I raised on the land a few tons of hay but since

> January 1899 for reasons stated above and by reason of drought of least 4 years I have raised no vegetables no produces of any kind. During this time I have had no other property of any description and have had no income from any source but my pension. This has been totally insufficient to provide me with the necessities of life and I sold 6 acres of my land for $30 and some apples this month to our support. During this time I have also had help from my sons who are in the main thought for my supplies and I wouldn't have suffered for the necessities of life. I do not claim the increased rating prior to January 1-1899 being now unable to defend such likely to come.
>
> In addition to my service in Co A. Mormon Battalion for the U.S. I also served during The Walker Indian War 1850–1853 under Capt Orville Cox and in the Black Hawk War of 1865–1867 under Capt. J.T.S. Allred (myself capt.) The services named are all Military in Nature ever rendered by me. I had but 58 acres in 1901. If 68 acres occurs in the assets in my records it is an error; and I do not know why 58 acres are listed against me in 1902 for I had sold 6 acres in 1901 leaving but 52 acres.

In 1897, a Pioneer Jubilee was held celebrating the 50th Anniversary of the pioneers coming to the Salt Lake Valley. Original wagons and pioneers who had driven those wagons participated in a parade. Pioneers were contacted for comments to include in the semi centennial publication, *The Book of the Pioneers: A Record of those who arrived in the Valley of the Great Salt during the year 1847*. They were also asked for relics to include for exhibition in the Deseret Museum. James T.S. Allred wrote, "I would like to keep my gun if you do not insist that I should give it to the State."

*

James T.S. Allred died March 29, 1905, in Spring City, Utah. The inscription on his tombstone is framed by carved rooftops:

Death is The Crown of Life
In my Father's House Are Many Mansions

Mormon Church historian Andrew Jenson wrote the following biography of James T.S. Allred in 1898:

> The oldest inhabitant of Spring City, son of James and Elizabeth Allred, was born in Bedford Co., Tenn., March 28, 1825. The family removed to Monroe Co., Mo., in 1830, joined the Mormon Church in 1832, moved to Clay Co., in 1835, to Caldwell Co in 1836, and in 1839, they were driven out with the Mormons to Pittsfield, Pike Co., Ill., thence to Nauvoo. On February 7, 1846, father and two brothers started West and on May 20th, James followed with three brothers meeting at Pisgah.
>
> At Council Bluffs, James enlisted in the Mormon Battalion in Company A. They went to Santa Fe, from which place, he and others returned to Pueblo on detached service, and in 1847, again started West, under Capt. James Brown, reaching Salt Lake City, July 29th, where he was discharged. He went to making adobes, but was called to help settle Sanpete. In May, 1849, he was sent with ten others, by President Young, to construct a bridge across the Platte River. They ferried teams at $4 each wagon, at the rate of seventy per day. He cleared $1,000 and returned to Salt Lake City with an outfit of two wagons, four yoke of oxen, four cows and a heifer, with all kinds of merchandise picked up on the river, having been left by emigrants. He brought a good supply of seed wheat, which was taken to Manti in Capt. Isaac Morley's company of 30, which reached there in

November, 1849. He also took a whip-saw and sawed lumber there and in other settlements. The first winter was severe, and he lost nine head of stock and fed most of his seed wheat. On March 22, 1852, he and father and their families, came to Spring City, being the first on the ground. He brought a log house ready to put up, and erected it the first day, covering with boards. The company consisted of James, his wife, and two children, father, his wife and son Andrew J., three grandchildren and Charles Whitlock, Geo. M. Allred and James F. Allred, with an Indian boy and girl he had bought from the Utes. Others came in the fall. On July 29, 1853, they lost all their stock and had to return to Manti on account of Indians. In October, they returned to Spring City, but had to leave again December 17th. On February 4, 1854, they went to Ephraim and helped build a fort. In May, 1855, he was called to the Las Vegas Indian Mission as an interpreter, and remained two years, returning to Ephraim. In 1864, was called on an Indian Mission to Circle Valley, where he built a home and had many improvements, but was driven out in June, 1866, and returned to Ephraim. Came to Spring City again in July, 1866, built a home, received some land, and now has 73 acres. He served as Major in the Black Hawk War, and was Captain of Minutemen in Spring City. Was Road Superviser one term, Selectman for several years. Was first councellor to Bishop of Ephraim and Spring City, Bishop R.N. Allred, was second councellor to Bishop C.G. Edwards at Ephraim. Was also County and City Surveyor for several years. His first wife was Eliza B. Mainwaring. She has eight living children: Eliza B., Ellen E., Elizabeth D., James T.S., Edward F., William H., Brigham Y., and Margaret B. Second wife was Margaret Mainwaring. She has four children: Malinda, Lovina S., Heber K., and Barbara, all

> married. Third wife was Purlina J. Coy. She is the only wife living. His progeny now number 120.

The omission of his marriage to Fanny Shantaquint is noteworthy given the practise of meticulous record keeping.

*

March is an unsettled month in the high mountain valley where Spring City rests. The violets are in bloom. The lilies of the valley are bursting through the moist earth. The days are getting longer. The soft pink light throws its shadows on the earth. The willows are purple. The lambs are being born. Spring snowstorms dust the mountains and the backs of the newborn lambs. The sunsets come full blown purple with a wash of grey.

A fragrant blood red peony my grandmother planted, which was taken off of a start from the garden of my great grandparents, still blooms in the yard of our family home in Spring City, Utah.

My father says that his knees hurt him. He says he would like to play another game of baseball. When he was young and living on the farm in Spring City, Utah, his younger brother Cy and he would play baseball. They would pretend to be playing in the major leagues. My father would pretend to be the Giant's left handed pitcher, Carl Hubble, and Cy would pretend to be Lefty Gomez, the Yankee's left handed pitcher. Both were right handed. They would play pitch and catch with one another out in the field where the hay grew north of the house. My father would pretend to be the Giant's outfielder Mel Ott when he was not pitching.

My Grandma loved a good story. She often told me, "You see we lived right here and grandpa, why he lived just on the corner and we'd have ta go clear round the block ta get home there were so many Indians sleeping on the porch and in the yard. You see he could talk the Indian talk and that's why they'd come ya see, ta get something ta eat.

Why they'd be clear round the block and I think if they'd treated the Indians right in the first place there wouldn't a been so much trouble…"

Chronology

March 28, 1825—James Tillman Sanford Allred, fifth son, tenth of twelve children, is born Farmington, Bedford County, Tennessee, to James and Elizabeth Allred.

1830—The Allred Family moves to Salt River, Ralls County, Missouri (Ralls County was later divided becoming Ralls County and Monroe County, Missouri).

September 10, 1832—James and Elizabeth Allred baptized into the Mormon Church by George Hinkle.

September 1835—James Allred and family, with brothers Isaac and William Allred families, move to Clay County, Missouri.

February 22, 1835—James T.S. Allred baptized into the Mormon Church by William O. Clark.

1837—The Allred Family moves to Caldwell County, Missouri, where James Allred is elected County Judge.

Spring 1839—The Allred Family moves to Pittsfield, Pike County, Illinois after the Mormons are driven from Missouri.

Fall 1839—The Allred Family moves to Commerce, Illinois, later named Nauvoo, Illinois.

1842—James T.S. Allred ordained into the 4th Quorum of the Seventies, an office in the priesthood of Mormon Church.

1842—Fanny Shantaquint Allred, a member of the Ute Indian Tribe is born in the area surrounding Sanpete County, Utah.

June 27, 1844—Joseph and Hyrum Smith murdered in Carthage, Illinois. September 28, 1844—James T.S. Allred registered as 1st Lieutenant in the Nauvoo Legion in the Hancock County Militia.

May 24, 1845—James T.S. Allred is present at the laying of the capstone on the Nauvoo Temple, in Nauvoo, Illinois.

November 23, 1845—James T.S. Allred marries Eliza Bridget Mainwaring.

February 9, 1846—James T.S. and Eliza Allred cross the Mississippi River after leaving Nauvoo, Illinois, when persecution of the Mormons intensifies.

July 15, 1846—James T.S. and Eliza Allred arrive at the Missouri River.

July 16, 1846—James T.S. Allred joins the Mormon Battalion as a private in Company A. Eliza accompanies him on this journey as a laundress and a cook.

July 21, 1846—James T.S. and Eliza Allred begin the march west with the Mormon Battalion.

August 1, 1846—Mormon Battalion arrives in Fort Leavenworth, Kansas where they are equipped with firearms, gear and draw their pay of $42.

August 12–14, 1846—Battalion leaves Fort Leavenworth for Santa Fe, New Mexico.

September 8, 1846—Fent F. Allred is born and dies en route to Santa Fe, New Mexico and Pueblo, Colorado to James T.S. and Eliza Allred, Allred catches up with the Company late at night exhausted after burying the infant.

November 17, 1846—James T.S. and Eliza Allred arrive in Pueblo, Colorado with a detachment of those too sick to continue on with the Mormon Battalion.

May 24, 1847—James T.S. and Eliza Allred cross the Arkansas River traveling north to meet the Mormon Battalion near Fort Laramie.

June 16, 1847—The Company camps near Fort Laramie.

July 24, 1847—Mormon pioneers found Salt Lake City as the first city of the State of Deseret.

July 29, 1847—James T.S. and Eliza Allred arrive in Salt Lake City, Utah. He is discharged from the Mormon Battalion upon arriving in Salt Lake City. He begins to make adobes. The Allred Family settles at the mouth of Big Cottonwood Canyon near Big Cottonwood Creek.

February 2 1848—Treaty of Guadalupe Hidalgo signed by the U.S. and Mexico granting the region of Deseret to the U.S.

February 28, 1848—Eliza Marie Allred is born in Salt Lake City, Utah to James T.S. and Eliza Allred.

May 1849—James T.S. Allred is Captain of the 2nd Company of the 2nd Battalion of the 1st Regiment of the Nauvoo Legion commanded by Daniel H. Wells.

May, June and July 1849—James T.S. Allred along with ten others returns to the Platte River to establish a ferry charging $4 a team and ferrying seventy teams a day. He returns with $1,000 and other goods, including two wagons, four yoke of oxen, four cows, a heifer and seed wheat.

November 22, 1849—James T.S. and Eliza Allred move to Manti, Utah with thirty families to help begin a new settlement.

January 13, 1850—Ellen Aurelia Allred is born in Manti, Utah to James T.S. and Eliza Allred.

October 1851—James and Elizabeth Allred arrive in Manti after a five-year separation, re-joining James T.S. and Eliza Allred.

1852 Plural marriage publicly announced in Salt Lake City (published in Doctrine and Covenants in 1876).

March 22, 1852—James T.S. and Eliza Allred, their two daughters, Eliza Marie and Ellen Aurelia, their adopted Indian boy, Nephi Allred and Reuben Warren Allred's adopted Indian Girl, Rachel Allred, move to "The Allred Settlement", later called Spring City, Utah.

March 25, 1852—Elizabeth Diantha Allred is born in Manti, Utah to James T.S. and Eliza Allred.

March 28, 1853—James T.S. Allred ordained Second Counselor to Bishop Reuben Warren Allred by Brigham Young.

July 29, 1853—James T.S. and Eliza Allred evacuate Spring City, Utah after losing all their stock in an Indian raid and return to Manti, Utah.

October 1853—James T.S. Allred and family, ten additional Allred families and forty Danish families return to Spring City, Utah.

December 17, 1853—Spring City is evacuated second time due to conflict with local Indians. James T.S. Allred is post commander. The Allred's, as well as other settlers, return to Manti, Utah.

October 1853—Party of Captain John Gunnison massacred near Fillmore.

February 25, 1854—James Tillman Sanford Allred Junior is born in Manti, Utah to James T.S. and Eliza Allred.

February 4, 1854—James T.S. and Eliza Allred move to settle Ephraim, Utah.

May 12, 1854—Walker War ends. Brigham Young and Chief Wakara make peace settlement.

April 6, 1855—James T.S. Allred called by Brigham Young to go on an Indian mission to Las Vegas, Nevada serving as an interpreter.

May 8, 1855—James T.S. Allred, Reuben Allred and Charles Whitlock and Company of U.S. soldiers leave Ephraim, Utah. James T.S. Allred serves as an interpreter for the military.

May 13, 1855—James T.S. Allred leaves the military company.

May 29, 1855—James T.S. Allred joins the missionaries bound for Las Vegas at the Iron Works west of Cedar City, Utah.

June 16, 1855—James T.S. Allred and Mormon party arrive in Las Vegas, Nevada.

November 10, 1855—James T.S. Allred leaves Las Vegas, Nevada to return to Ephraim, Utah.
November 26, 1855—James T.S. Allred arrives in Ephraim, Utah.

April 12, 1856—James T.S. Allred marries Margaret Mainwaring Roberts.

May 29, 1856—James T.S. Allred and families arrive at Las Vegas, Nevada.

September 5, 1856—Edward Francis Allred is born in Las Vegas, Nevada to James T.S. and Eliza Allred. He is blessed by William S. Covert, William Bringhurst and by his father James T.S. Allred.

February 11, 1857—Sarah Ann Allred is born in Las Vegas, Nevada to James T.S. and Margaret Allred.

February 23, 1857—Brigham Young releases missionaries serving Las Vegas, Nevada and encourages their return home. Most leave within the month.

March 4, 1857—President James Buchanan takes office.

March 18, 1857—James T.S. Allred and wives Eliza and Margaret return to Ephraim, Utah.

Sometime after March 18, 1857—James T.S. Allred marries Fanny Shantaquint a member of the Ute Indian Tribe.

April 1857—United States troops mobilized at Fort Douglas.

June 29, 1857—President James Buchanan declares Utah in rebellion against the U.S. government.

September 11, 1857—Mountain Meadows massacre.

April 12, 1858—Brigham Young surrenders title of governor to Alfred Cumming.

October 5, 1858—John Richard Allred is born in Ephraim, Utah to James T.S. and Margaret Allred, but dies the following day.
November 4, 1858—William Hackley Allred is born in Ephraim, Utah to James T.S. and Eliza Allred.

February 14, 1860—Barbara Allred is born in Ephraim, Utah, to James T.S. and Fanny Allred.

February 9, 1861—Malinda Jane Allred is born in Ephraim, Utah to James T.S. and Margaret Allred.

April 12, 1861—American Civil War begins (1861–1865).

April 14, 1861—Nancy Cluny Allred is born in Ephraim, Utah to James T.S. and Eliza Allred.

October 1861—First transcontinental telegraph completed. Salt Lake City is the last link.

August 25, 1862—Brigham Young Allred is born in Ephraim, Utah to James T.S. and Eliza Allred.

December 13, 1862—James T.S. Allred is sealed to Fanny Shantaquint.

January 29, 1863—Bear River massacre. Five hundred and thirty-one Shoshone killed by United States Army.

April 9, 1863—Lovina Smith Allred is born in Ephraim, Utah to James T.S. and Margaret Allred.

December 1863—James T.S. Allred, James Munson and Andrew Jackson Allred and a party of four others arrive in Circle Valley from Ephraim to explore the suitability of a establishing a settlement on the Sevier River.

March 1864—They obey Brigham Young's call to establish a settlement although having reservations about the size and isolation of the site.

1864—Jacob Allred is born and dies in Ephraim, Utah to James T.S. and Fanny Allred.

April 8, 1865—Chief Jake Arapeen and John Lowry fight in Manti, Utah. Considered the beginning of the Black Hawk War.

November 26, 1865 Ute Warriors attack settlers traveling back to Circleville, Utah, killing four people. Most of the stock is driven off.

April 20, 1866—Margaret Bridget Allred is born in Circleville, Utah to James T.S. and Eliza Allred.

April 20, 1866—Eliza Bridget Mainwaring Allred dies in Circleville, Utah six hours after giving birth to infant daughter. She is buried the same day due to tense relations with local Indians.

April 22, 1866—Paiute Indians killed in Circleville, Utah in tragic massacre.

June 20, 1866—James T.S. Allred and others evacuate Circleville as Black Hawk War intensifies. They return to Ephraim.

July 1866—James T.S. and Margaret Allred return to Spring City, Utah. While living in Spring City, Allred serves as Captain of the Minutemen, City and County Surveyor, Road Supervisor, City Councilman, Cemetery Sexton and Mormon Bishop's Counselor.

October 1866—Hannah Allred is born and dies in Circleville, Utah to James T.S. and Fanny Allred.

November 1, 1866—Fanny Shantaquint Allred dies alone in Circleville, Utah.

May 3, 1868—Heber Kimball Allred is born in Spring City, Utah to James T.S. and Margaret Allred.

November 29, 1875—James T.S. Allred marries Perlina Jane Allred Coy Allred a widow and his brother, Reuben Warren Allred's daughter.

January 10, 1876—James Allred, father of James T.S. Allred dies in Spring City, Utah.

April 23, 1879—Elizabeth Warren Allred, mother of James T.S. Allred, dies in Spring City, Utah.

1882—*Edmunds Act* makes polygamy a punishable felony. Unlawful cohabitation becomes a misdemeanour punishable by a $300 fine and six months imprisonment.

1888—Margaret Mainwaring Roberts Allred is questioned on February 28, 1888 and the first week in October 1888 before a grand jury for unlawful cohabitation. The inclement weather on her journeys and the stress from the questioning compromise her health.

October 10, 1888—Margaret Mainwaring Roberts Allred dies in Spring City, Utah. Tombstone inscription: "A Tender Mother and Faithful Friend".

1890—Church President Wilford Woodruff issues a Manifesto that officially terminates the practice of polygamy.

March 28, 1905—James T.S. Allred's 80th birthday.

March 29, 1905—James T.S. Allred dies in Spring City, Utah.

March 31, 1905—Funeral held for James T.S. Allred.
Family tombstone inscription: "In My Fathers House Are Many Mansions".
Tombstone inscription: "Death Is The Crown of Life".

February 1, 1910—Perlina Jane Allred Coy Allred dies in Spring City, Utah.
Tombstone inscription: "Sheltered and Safe from Sorrow".

Allred Family Tree

I

THOMAS ALLRED

Born about 1730 Northumberland County, Virginia

ELIZABETH ALLRED

Born about 1732 in Randolph County, North Carolina. Children:

1. James Born about 1754
2. **William Born about 1756**
3. Elias Born May 6, 1758
4. John Born about 1760
5. Rachel Born about 1762
6. Moses Born about1764
7. Eli Born about 1766
8. Elizabeth Born about 1768
9. Thomas, Junior Born about 1775
10. Levi Born about 1777

II

WILLIAM ALLRED

Born about 1756 Randolph County, North Carolina

Died about 1824 Bedford County, Tennessee

Married about 1777

ELIZABETH THRASHER

Born about 1760 Randolph County, North Carolina

Died about 1841 Monroe County, Missouri

Children:

1. Sarah Allred 1781–1861
2. Mary Allred 1783–1820
3. **James Allred January 22, 1784–January 10, 1876**
4. Elizabeth Allred 1786
5. Isaac Allred 1788–1870
6. William Allred 1790–1841
7. Martha Allred 1792
8. John Allred 1794–1860

III

JAMES ALLRED

Born January 22, 1784 in Randolph County, North Carolina.

Died January 10, 1876 in Spring City, San Pete County, Utah.

Married November 14, 1803 in Franklin County, Georgia

ELIZABETH WARREN

Born May 6, 1786 in Spartanburg County, South Carolina.

Died April 23, 1879 in Rabbit Valley, Wayne County, Utah

Children:

1. William Hackley April 14, 1804–August 1, 1890
2. Martin Carrol September 8, 1806–May 2, 1840
3. Hannah Caroline September 20, 1808–February 23, 1850
4. Sally April 13, 1811–December 2, 1834
5. Isaac June 28, 1813–May 12, 1859
6. Reuben Warren November 18, 1815–October 4, 1896
7. Wiley Payne May 31, 1818–March 28, 1912
8. Nancy Chummy September 10, 1820–1842
9. Eliza Maria October 28, 1822–July 30, 1842
10. **James Tillman Sanford March 28, 1825–March 29, 1905**
11. John Franklin Lafayette June 26, 1827–July 17, 1847
12. Andrew Jackson February 12, 1831–October 10, 1899

Other Wives:

2. Sarah Warren Married January 28, 1846
3. Elizabeth Patrick Taylor Married February 3, 1846

IV

JAMES TILLMAN SANFORD ALLRED

Born March 28, 1825 in Farmington, Bedford County, Tennessee.

Died March 29, 1905 in Spring City, San Pete County, Utah.

Married November 23, 1845 in Nauvoo, Hancock County, Illinois

ELIZA BRIDGET MAINWARING

Born November 23, 1821 in Presteigne, Herefordshire, England.

Died April 20, 1866 in Circleville, Paiute County, Utah.

Children:

1. Fent F. 1846 in Colorado

2. Eliza Marie February 28, 1848–April 12, 1939
3. Ellen Aurelia January 13, 1850–August 29, 1929
4. Elizabeth Diantha March 25, 1852–September 24, 1942
5. James Tillman Sanford, Jr., February 25, 1854–August 11, 1903
6. Edward Francis September 5, 1856–July 9, 1942
7. William Hackley November 4, 1858—February 15, 1922
8. Nancy Cluny April 14, 1861–April 14, 1861
9. Brigham Young August 25, 1862–September 24, 1949
10. Margaret Bridget April 20, 1866–August 4, 1934

Other Wives:

MARGARET MAINWARING ROBERTS
Born December 10, 1820 Presteign, Hertfordshire, England
Died October 10, 1888 in Spring City, Sanpete County, Utah
Married April 12, 1856
Children:

1. Sarah Ann Allred Born February 11, 1857 in Las Vegas, Nevada
2. John Richard Allred October 5- 6, 1858 in Ephraim, Utah
3. Malinda Jane Allred Born February 9, 1861 in Ephraim, Utah
4. Lovina Smith Allred Born April 9, 1863 in Ephraim, Utah
5. Heber Kimball Allred Born May 3,1868 in Spring City, Utah

FANNY SHANTAQUINT
Born March 4, 1842
Died November 1, 1866 Circleville, Sevier County, Utah
Married 1857. Sealed December 13, 1862.
Children:

1. Barbara Allred Born February 14, 1858 in Ephraim, Utah
2. Jacob Allred Born and dies in 1864 in Ephraim, Utah
3. Hannah Allred Born and dies October 1866 in Circleville, Utah

PERLINA JANE ALLRED COY
Born May 17, 1833 Monroe County, Missouri
Died February 1, 1910, Spring City, Sanpete County, Utah
Married November 29, 1875

V

EDWARD FRANCIS ALLRED
Born September 5, 1856 in Las Vegas, Clark County, Nevada.
Died July 9, 1942 in Spring City, Sanpete County, Utah
SALLY BILLINGTON
Born July 16, 1860 Adair County, Missouri
Died May 5, 1882 in Spring City, Sanpete County,Utah
Married November 17, 1880
Children:

1. Edna April 9, 1882- August 18, 1943

ELIZABETH OVERLADE
Born October 27, 1861 in Ephraim, Sanpete County, Utah
Died February 10, 1935 in Spring City, Sanpete County, Utah
Married October 2, 1884
Children:

1. Sarah July 2, 1885- January 3, 1975
2. Edward Francis, Junior, August 1, 1886- June 12, 1887
3. Aurelia Andrear, January 17, 1888–November 6, 1938
4. Ethelyn Dorcas, January 5, 1890- October 28, 1967
5. **Carried LaFern, April 11, 1896–December 28, 1982**
6. Leah Helene, October 1, 1902–August 17, 1987

VI

CARRIE LAFERN ALLRED
Born April 11, 1896 in Spring City, Sanpete County, Utah.
Died December 28, 1982 in Spring City, Sanpete County, Utah.
Married March 27, 1918 in Spring City, Sanpete County, Utah

DANIEL LAMONT JENSEN
Born August 7, 1893 in Spring City, Sanpete County, Utah.
Died March 13, 1969 in Spring City, Sanpete County, Utah.
Children:

1. Neldon Lamont February 22, 1925–February 24, 2010

2. Lavar March 5, 1927–December 9, 1988

VII
NELDON LAMONT JENSEN
Born February 22, 1925 in Spring City, Sanpete County, Utah
Died February 24, 2010 in Spring City, Utah
Married December 18, 1946 in Ephraim, Sanpete County, Utah.

KATHLEEN PAULSEN HINCKLEY JENSEN
Born January 12, 1922 in Ephraim, Utah
Died March 10, 2009 in Spring City, Utah
Children:

1. Carol Hinckley Sjoborg February 10, 1944 in Ephraim, Sanpete County, Utah

2. Sue August 8, 1948 in Provo, Utah County, Utah

3. Robert Lamont March 13, 1953 in Salt Lake City, Salt Lake County, Utah

Jensen Family Tree

I

DANIEL JOHANSEN

Born about 1748 in Helsingor, Denmark

Married SOPHIE LARSEN

Born about 1745 in Helsingor, Denmark

Children:

1. Marie Margrethe January 1, 1784
2. **Jens November 19, 1802–December 24, 1834**
3. Cecilia Christine December 31, 1789

II

JENS DANIELSEN

Born November 19, 1802 Helsingor, Fredericksborg, Denmark

Died December 24, 1834

Married

ANNE KIRSTINE OLSEN

Born February 7, 1808 Gunnerod, Fredericksborg, Denmark

Died 1877

Children:

1. Daniel
2. Anders February 13, 1831
3. **Niels Peter**

III

NIELS PETER

Born December 31, 1833 Sannde, Fredericksborg, Denmark

Married

ELLEN MARIE RASMUSSEN

Born June 10, 1842 in Norre, Snede, Denmark

Died April 14, 1952 in Spring City Sanpete County, Utah

Children:

1. **Daniel July 14, 1865- April 14, 1952**
2. Kirstine March 27, 1867- April 22, 1867

3. Christine March 5, 1869- February 14, 1955

4. Laure Line January 2, 1872- March 25, 1950 - **Married David Monson**

5. Louise March 23, 1873- September 14, 1873

6. Rasmine August 8, 1874- July 27, 1955

7. Andrew July 4, 1876- October 20, 1918

IV

DANIEL JENSEN

Born July 14, 1865 in Jorring, Skanderborg, Denmark

Died April 14, 1952 in Spring City, Sanpete County, Utah

Married January 21, 1892

MARGARET ALICE BLAIN

Born January 29, 1870 in Spring City, Sanpete County, Utah

Died October 18, 1895 in Spring City, Sanpete County, Utah

Children:

1. Daniel Lamont Jensen

Born August 7, 1893 in Spring City, Sanpete County, Utah

Died March 13, 1969 in Spring City, Sanpete County, Utah

Other Wives:

2. Jo Hannah B. Nielson February 9, 1858- August 27, 1929

3. Methe Larsen November 22, 1880- June 15, 1944

4. Anna Wilhelmina B. Billington May 26, 1870- December 19, 1955

Bibliography

Allred, Donald Clemont. Allred Family Roster Update. Allred Family Newsletter. October 1990, Issue #35.

Allred, Donald Clemont. Allred Family Roster Update. Allred Family Newsletter. Summer 1998, Issue #37.

Allred, Elizabeth Diantha, Elizabeth Diantha Allred. Unpublished Autobiography.

Allred, Newton. Newton Allred. Unpublished Autobiography. Salt Lake City, Utah. Utah State Historical Society.

Allred, William H. Letter to George A. Smith, May 5, 1866. The Church Of Jesus Christ Of Latter Day Saints Historical Department, Salt Lake City, Utah.

Allen, Carrie. History of Circleville. Richfield, Utah, Reaper Press, 1966.

Antrei, Albert. High, Dry and Offside. Manti, Utah, Manti City Corporation, 1995.

Antrei, Albert C.T. and Roberts, Allen D. A History of Sanpete County. Salt Lake City, Utah, Utah State Historical Society, 1999.

Basler, Roy P. Abraham Lincoln: His Speeches and Writings. Cleveland, Ohio, The World Publishing Company, 1946.

Bean, George W. The Journal of George W. Bean Las Vegas Springs, New Mexico Territory, 1856–1857. Edited by Harry C. Dees. Nevada Historical Quarterly. Volume XV No. 3, Fall 1972.

Brooks, Juanita. Indian Relations on the Mormon Frontier. Utah Historical Quarterly. Volume 12, 1948, pp. 1–48.

Campbell, Eugene E. Brigham Young's Outer Cordon—A Reappraisal. Utah Historical Quarterly. Volume 41, No. 3, 1973, pp. 220–253.

Carter, Kate B. Our Pioneer Heritage. Salt Lake City, Utah, Daughters of the Utah Pioneers. Volume 9, 1966.

Christy, Howard A. The Walker War: Defense and Conciliation as Strategy. Utah Historical Quarterly. Volume 47, No. 4, 1979, pp. 395–420.

Circleville Ward History. Church of Jesus Christ of Latter Day Saints Historical Department, Salt Lake City, Utah.

Cooley, D.N. Letter March 14, 1866. Church of Jesus Christ of Latter Day Saints Historical Department, Salt Lake City, Utah.

Conetah, Fred A. A History of the Northern Ute People. Uintah—Ouray Ute Tribe, University of Utah, 1982.

Culmsee, Carlton. Utah's Black Hawk War: Lore and Reminiscences of Participants. Logan, Utah State University Press, 1973.

Davidson, James West and Stoff, Michael B. The American Nation. Englewood Cliffs, New Jersey, 1995.

DeLafosse, Peter H. Trailing the Pioneers: A Guide to Utah's Emigrant Trails 1829–1869. Logan, Utah, Utah State University Press, 1994.

DeVoto, Bernard. Across the Wide Missouri. New York: Houghton Mifflin, 1975.

DeVoto, Bernard. 1846, The Year of Decision. Boston: Houghton Mifflin, 1960.

Durham, Michael S. Desert Between The Mountains: Mormons, Miners, Padres, Mountain Men, And The Opening Of The Great Basin, 1772–1869. New York, Henry Holt and Company, 1997.

Dees, Harry C. The Journal of George W. Bean Las Vegas Springs, New Mexico Territory, 1856–1857. Nevada Historical Quarterly Volume 41, No. 3, Fall 1972.

Ephraim's First One Hundred Years 1854- 1954. Centennial Book Committee, 1954.

Fish, Joseph. The Life and Times of Joseph Fish, Mormon pioneer. Danville, Illinois, Interstate Printers & Publishers, 1970.

Gardner, Hamilton. Pioneer Military Leaders of Utah. Salt Lake City, Utah. self publication, 1952.

Gottfredson, Peter. Indian Depredations of Utah. 1919. Salt Lake City, Utah. Press of Skelton Publishing Co., 1919.

Jensen, Emil J. History of the Chester Ward Sanpete County, Utah 1870–1964. The Church of Jesus Christ of Latter Day Saints Genealogical Society.

Jensen, Louis, Unpublished Family Records. Salt Lake City, Utah.

Jenson, Andrew. History of the Las Vegas Mission April 1855. The Church of Jesus Christ of Latter Day Saints Historical Department, Salt Lake City, Utah.

Jenson, Andrew. James T.S. Allred 1898. The Church of Jesus Christ of Latter Day Saints Historical Department, Salt Lake City, Utah.

Johnson, Linda Hansen. Unpublished Family Records. Spring City, Utah.

Larsen, Eunice D. Biography of Ellen Aurelia Allred Nielsen. Marysvale, Utah, Alunite Mill, June 15, 1919. Unpublished biography.

Larson, Oluf C. A Biographical Sketch of the Life of Oluf Christian Larsen Dictated by himself and written by his son Oluf Larsen, Dedicated to his posterity who might desire to read it. 1916. Church of Jesus Christ of Latter Day Saints Historical Department Salt Lake City, Utah.

Leavitt, Francis H. The Influence of the Mormon People in the Settlement of Clark County. Las Vegas, University of Nevada, 1934.

Longsdorf, Hilda Madsen. Mount Pleasant 1859–1939. Salt Lake City, Utah, Utah Stevens and Wallis Inc., 1939.

Ludlow, Daniel H. Encyclopedia of Mormonism, Volume 3. New York, Macmillan Publishing Company, 1992.

Lund, Jennifer L. Unpublished Family Records. Salt Lake City, Utah.

Lyman, June and Denver, Norma. Ute People An Historical Study.
Salt Lake City, Utah, Uintah School District and the Western History Center, 1970.

Martineau, Levan. The Southern Paiutes: Legends, Lore, Language and Lineage. Nevada, KC Publications, 1992.

Meltzer, Milton. Mark Twin Himself: A Pictorial Biography. New York City, New York, Bonanza Books, 1960.

Mimms, Bob. Mormon Battalion Never Met Its Foe, But It Still Won A Mighty Victory. Salt Lake City, Utah, The Salt Lake Tribune, November 6, 1999.

Munson, Eliza Marie Allred. Early Pioneer History. Unpublished Autobiography.

Munson, Eliza Marie Allred. Questions Concerning Black Hawk War Answered by Eliza M. Munson. Utah State Historical Society, UWPA Project.

Nielsen, Ellen Aurelia Allred. Ellen Aurelia Allred Nielsen. Unpublished Autobiography.

Parker, Keith. A History of Presteigne. Herefordshire, England, Logaston Press, 1997.

Peterson, Gary B. and Bennion, Lowell C. Sanpete Scenes A Guide to Utah's Heart. Eureka,Utah, Basin Plateau Press, 1987.

Peterson, John Alton, Utah's Black Hawk War. Salt Lake City, University of Utah Press, 1998.

Pyper, Tessie. Rachel's Warning. Allred Family Newsletter Oct. Issue #5, 1990. Unpublished Family Records.

Quinn, Michael D. The Mormon Hierarchy: Extensions of Power. Salt Lake City, Signature Books, 1997.

Raber, Michael Scott. Spring City, Utah: Origins of a Mormon Town. New Haven, Yale University Press, 1978.

Rice, Cindy. Spring City: A Look at a Nineteenth-Century Mormon Village. Utah Historical Quarterly Volume 43, No 3, 1975, pp. 260–277.

Ricketts, Norma Baldwin. The Mormon Battalion. Logan, Utah, Utah State University Press, 1996.

Smith, Joseph, translator. The Book of Mormon. Salt Lake City, Utah, The Church of Jesus Christ of Latter Day Saints, 1981.

Spencer, Diana Majors. Editor. The Other 49ers: A topical history of Sanpete County Utah. Salt Lake City, Utah, Western Epics, 1982.

Smith, George Albert, Letters 1817–1875. Church Of Jesus Christ of Latter Day Saints Historical Department, Salt Lake City, Utah.

Spencer, Deloy. The Utah Black Hawk War 1865–1871. Logan, Utah State University Press, 1969.

Steel, Linda Allred. James and Elizabeth Allred. Salt Lake City, Utah, Publishers Press, 1995.

Steele, John. Extracts from the Journal of John Steele. Utah Historical Quarterly Volume 6, No. 1, 1933, pp. 2–28.

Stegner, Wallace. The Gathering of Zion. New York, McGraw–Hill, 1964.

Stegner, Wallace. Mormon Country. Lincoln, Nebraska, University of Nebraska Press, 1970.

Thatcher, Linda. The Book of the Pioneers. Beehive History, No. 22, 1996, p. 13.

The Home Sentinel, Reminiscences of the Early Days of Manti. Utah Historical Quarterly. Volume 6, No. 4, Oct 1933, pp.117–123.

Tolton, Mary and John. Autobiography. Salt Lake City, Utah, Daughters of the Utah Pioneers Library.

Tolton, John Franklin. From The Halls of Memory. Salt Lake City, Utah, Utah State Historical Society.

Turner, Jackson Frederick. The Frontier in American History. New York, Dover Publications, Inc., 1996.

United States Government. House Ex. Docs. No.101, 39th Congress, 1st Session Volume XXI. Report on Expenses of the Indian Service, May 4, 1866.

United States Government. House of Representatives 39th Congress, 1st Session. Report No. 96. The Condition of Utah, July 23, 1866.

United States Government. House Misc. Docs. No 37, 39th Congress, 2nd Session, Volume I. Report on Indian Affairs, January 25, 1867.

United States Government. House of Representatives 1st Congress, 1st Session, Mis. Doc. No. 19, March 22, 1869.

Verdoia, Ken and Firmage, Richard. Utah: The Struggle for Statehood. Salt Lake City, University of Utah Press, 1996.

Ward, Geoffrey C. The West: An Illustrated History. New York City, New York, Little Brown and Company, 1996.

Watson, Kaye C. Life Under Horseshoe: A History of Spring City. Salt Lake City, Publishers Press, 1986.

Wells, Daniel H. Daniel H. Wells' Narrative. Utah Historical Quarterly. Volume 6, No. 4, 1933, pp.124–132.

Winkler, Albert. The Circleville Massacre: A Brutal Incident in Utah's Black Hawk War. Utah Historical Quarterly. Volume 55, No.1, 1987, pp.4–21.

Winkler, Albert. Justice in the Black Hawk War: The Trial of Thomas Jose. Utah Historical Quarterly. Volume 60, No. 2, 1992, pp. 124–136.

Winkler, Albert. The Ute Mode of War in The Conflict of 1865–68 Utah Historical Quarterly. Volume 60, No. 4, 1992, pp. 300–318.

Young, Brigham. Letter, Great Salt Lake City, Utah to Wm. H. Dame July 23, 1858. Church of Jesus Christ of Latter Day Saints Historical Department, Salt Lake City, Utah.

Young, Lorenzo Dow. Diary of Lorenzo Dow Young. Utah Historical Quarterly. Volume 14, No. 1,2,3,4, 1946, pp. 133–170.

Acknowledgments

I am grateful to the following people, resources and organizations:

Gordon Thompson, my publisher at Clouds of Magellan Press, without whom this book would not have been possible. Helen Bell, assistant editor, who with great care proofread this book.

Athene Osborne, Lila Allred, Suzanne Brady, Linda Allred Steele, Donna Pyper, Kaye Watson, Connell Osborne, Glen Osborne, Michael Scott Raber, Howard Christy, Dortha B. Davenport, Linda H. Johnson, Jenny Lund, George Whittaker, Becky Whittaker, Shane Robinson, Norma Baldwin Ricketts, Ann Edwards Cannon, Angela Meacham, Lois MacAllister, Connie A. Bergstedt, Albert Winkler, John Alton Peterson.

Allred Family Organization: Alice Allred Pottmyer, Larry C. Allred, Kathy Allred, Robert G. Blakely.

Daughters of the Utah Pioneers, Desert Valley Museum, Hansen Planetarium, University of Utah Special Collections, The Church of Jesus Christ of Latter Day Saints, Utah State Archives, Utah Historical Society, National Archives.

Paiute Elders: Lora Tom, Arthur and Phyllis Richards, Dorena Martineau, Ralph Pikyavit.

I am especially grateful to my father, Neldon Lamont Jensen, who spent countless hours scouring cemeteries, calling relatives and searching his memory ensuring a more interesting and accurate historical narrative.

www.ingramcontent.com/pod-product-compliance
Ingram Content Group UK Ltd.
Pitfield, Milton Keynes, MK11 3LW, UK
UKHW041629190726
13854UKWH00006B/2394

9 781742 984681